GIRL FRIDAY
TO GLADYS AYLWARD

Vera Cowie
GIRL FRIDAY TO
GLADYS AYLWARD

Best wishes,

Vera Cowie

LAKELAND
MARSHALL, MORGAN & SCOTT
A member of the Pentos group

1 Bath Street
LONDON ECIV 9QA

Copyright © Vera Cowie 1976
First published 1976
ISBN 0 551 00763 X

The names of some of the Chinese characters in this book have been changed to save any possible embarrassment.

Printed in Great Britain by
Cox & Wyman Ltd,
London, Reading and Fakenham
676003R51

Contents

Illustrations

Acknowledgments

I should like to thank my relatives and friends for taking care of the on-the-spot tape recordings I made of day-to-day happenings in Taiwan and for allowing me the use of letters which I sent to them. Without these I would not have been able to give such an accurate picture of life in the Children's Home in Taiwan.

I should also like to thank Miss Lillie Hocking for offering to type my manuscript over a period of many months and for doing it so gladly and efficiently.

My thanks are also due to many other people – The Free Chinese Centre, London who kindly supplied me with books and maps of Taiwan to enable me to verify facts relating to the island; Mrs. Jean Rees, Major and Mrs. W. Ian Thomas, Mr. and Mrs. G. Greenwood, Mr. G. L. and the late Mrs. Manson, The Rev. Harry Palliser, Mr. Brian Chilver, Mr. N. Skene, Mr. Val Grieve, Mr. D. Davies, Jnr. and Mr. and Mrs. A. S. N. Foster for so kindly reading my manuscript and giving me their constructive comments; my publisher for being willing to accept my first attempt at writing; and most of all my thanks to God for giving me such a wonderful family, for without the loving co-operation and encouragement of my husband, I would never have found time to write this book.

Adopt a child — adopt a destiny!

When Pharaoh's daughter took th'abandoned babe from
    out the reeds,
I doubt she dreamed the grand design of Moses' deeds,
Nor could she guess the part she all unwittingly had played;
In helping man, she rendered great Jehovah aid!

Did Mordecai, as he watched the maiden Esther grow,
Her future fame foretell, or did he dimly know
That his fair charge would one day come to be great Xerxes'
    queen;
The once adopted orphan hailed as heroine!

What mighty rivers sometimes start from very smallest
    streams,
What great fulfilments followed favoured Joseph's dreams;
And who could guess, unless they knew, that oaks from
    acorns grew,
Or what adoption's blessings for a child can do?

ARTHUR MEE

1
'I want a Daddy.'

Three-and-a-half-year old Jade came running in from the garden.

'Kafryn says I haven't got a Daddy. Why not?'

The solemn, brown almond-shaped eyes of my adopted daughter looked up at me, waiting for the answer.

What could I say? Quickly I took her on my knee and explained that some boys and girls have a Mummy and Daddy but some don't have either. We were very fortunate to have each other. She had at least got a Mummy.

Ignoring the explanation, Jade said, 'But I want a Daddy.' Then her little face lit up. 'Why can't Uncle Jim be my Daddy?'

I laughed, knowing that the colour had come to my face but thankful that she had not even noticed.

'Well,' I said, 'it's a bit difficult. We can't really choose our own Daddy. But if we talk to God about it, then He might tell the right person.' Quick as a flash, Jade replied, 'Then why can't God tell Uncle Jim?'

Why not, indeed! Uncle Jim was a very important person in her life. She had first met this friend of mine when we visited Scotland, two or three weeks after our arrival home from Taiwan nearly two years ago. Since then he had never failed to send her something for Christmas.

That night, when she said her bedtime prayer she

remembered to add, 'And, dear Lord Jesus, please send me a Daddy, if you have one to spare.'

I was very touched by the simple faith of this small girl who, having chosen her own Mummy, had now decided that the time had come for her to have a Daddy, too. Jade was certainly following in the footsteps of her benefactor, the famous Miss Gladys Aylward, in whose children's home in Taiwan I had first met her.

As Jade lay blissfully sleeping, my own mind went back to the unforgettable adventures I had experienced with Gladys Aylward whose determination had taken her to mainland China some thirty years earlier; the discipline and privations of those intensely difficult early years preparing her for her epic trek across the mountains of China with almost a hundred orphans. Now, for the first time, one of her children had come to live in Britain (by special permission of the Queen) and this same child was here in my own tiny home; my own adopted daughter.

I thought of Gladys's first adopted child, also a girl, with the intriguing name of Ninepence, and how it had all begun. On one of Gladys's many treks into the mountains, she had come upon a woman sitting by the roadside with what looked like a bundle of rags in her lap. On closer inspection Gladys, whose insatiable curiosity had more than once landed her in difficult situations, discovered that the bundle contained a baby girl. The child was filthy and hardly recognisable as a human being. Angry questions tumbled over themselves as Gladys sought to control her emotions, while the woman just smiled in a slow aggravating way.

At last, she said, 'Do you want to buy the child? I don't want it. I can't be bothered with it,' noting with cruel amusement the devastating effect the child's pathetic condition was having on Gladys's feelings. 'If you don't take it, it will die,' she continued with the knowing

10

satisfaction that this soft-hearted Western woman would eventually give in. 'How much will you give me for it?'

'I have only ninepence,' said Gladys angrily.

'Ninepence will do,' replied the woman with glee and offered the smelly, filthy bundle to Gladys.

Without a word she gave the woman all the money she had and with warmth and satisfaction she clasped the child to her heart.

Little did Gladys know that Ninepence, as she called her, was to be only the first of a very large family. But then, my own meeting with this now famous 'Small Woman' had an equally profound effect on my own life ...

At the time I had a fulfilling job at Capernwray Hall, a holiday centre, situated in beautiful countryside just sixteen miles south of Kendal on the edge of the Lake District. This old hall had been taken over at the end of the war by two Christian army officers who had served in Europe: Major Ian Thomas and his colleague, Major Gordon Greenwood, and they invited speakers who would appeal to young people. Ian Thomas had met Gladys Aylward whilst lecturing in the south of England and was so impressed with the faith of the small dynamic woman that he invited her to visit us. Night after night staff and guests alike were entranced by the amazing stories she had to tell of her experiences on the mainland of China. She could speak for two hours and her audiences were captivated and waiting for more.

One evening during the first week of her visit, I made her acquaintance for the first time. I noticed her sitting alone reading a book. She seemed somewhat lonely and I had the urge to go over and ask whether there was anything I could do for her. I dismissed the urge, thinking, 'She has done so much in China and coped with such fantastic situations – she can't possibly need my help.' But the voice inside me persisted. So finally I went over to where she was sitting and said, 'Excuse me, Miss Aylward, but I wondered whether there was anything I could do for you – perhaps letters or something?'

Her face lit up as she looked up at me and said, 'How wonderful – I've been asking God to send someone to help me with letters. I have so many and can't possibly reply to them all myself.'

So began our working partnership. Ian Thomas had suggested that she make Capernwray her 'headquarters' in the north of England. She gladly accepted the invitation and, whenever she appeared, out came the bundles of letters for me to help her with. At other times, she would just pack up the bundles and post them on to me with notes on each one – 'Say No – can't go' or 'Give them 26th October' or something similar.

Occasionally I would go to London for a weekend to stay with Gladys in a flat provided for her by some Christian friends. On one such visit I met Alan Burgess who was in the process of writing his book *The Small Woman* and had called in to see Gladys.

To my amazement she introduced me to him as 'My business manager – Miss Porter.' That was the first that I had heard of such a title and was secretly very amused. How could anyone 'manage' such a character? All I had done was to manage 'the letters', but Gladys obviously meant it as a compliment and I felt privileged to be her friend and helper, little realising what was ahead.

Gladys continued to visit us at Capernwray from time to time, and whenever we heard that she was coming back I would rush through the winding lanes in the big old shooting brake to pick her up at Carnforth station. In summer we would have afternoon tea on the big lawns outside the house, looking across the lovely gardens which were a riot of colour. Here young people would crowd around Gladys, eager to hear more stories of her life in the enchanting East which, in spite of the hardships, seemed to appear fascinating whenever Gladys told her stories. As she spoke her young audiences were out there with her – meeting bandits, rescuing small children, quelling prison riots and taking part in all the other wonderfully exciting things she had done.

Soon after Gladys had decided it was time for her to return to Taiwan, she came to visit us at Capernwray. As we talked about the future I suggested that we open a bank account for her at a local bank (my previous banking experience coming to the fore!). Then gifts could be sent to me, and I hoped the bank would see that they reached her via Hong Kong. Off we went to see the bank manager and he arranged everything in a matter of minutes.

We were very sad at the prospect of Gladys leaving, but realised that her heart was in the Far East. How could she settle away from her beloved Chinese people? We bade her 'God-speed', promising to keep in touch by letter.

Little did I know, as I waved goodbye to Gladys, that in the not-too-far-distant future I would be travelling out to the Far East with this little cockney ex-parlourmaid.

2
'This is Your Life'

In the next year or two letters arrived from the Far East, containing intriguing mementoes – lovely life-sized butterflies skilfully pressed into coloured leaves of all kinds, a coloured map showing the various products Taiwan had to offer by way of export or tourism, a beautiful jacket in Chinese silk with exquisite patterns of flowering trees, lakes and pagodas, conjuring up in my mind an alluring picture of life in that faraway place.

I was now working at Keele University, having left the youth centre, feeling that I should be at home for a short time after the death of my father. My mother and I were living with my sister and brother-in-law and I drove to the university offices each day.

But I felt life was becoming a bit dull. At the youth centre I had met young people from all over Europe, travelled to the Continent, opened an office in Germany and eventually seen a German youth centre in operation. Those had been exciting days! Yet, as I reasoned with myself, I knew that I was in the right place. Had I not asked God to guide me when I left the youth centre? Only that morning, 28th April, 1963, I had read on my desk calendar: 'Thy way is in the sea and Thy path in the great waters (Psalm 77: 19). God's path is in the sea – just where you would not expect it to be! So when He leads us out by unexpected ways, off the strong solid land, out upon the *changing* sea, *then* we may expect to see His *ways*. We are with One who finds a path as He goes.

There is an infinite variety in the paths God makes and He can make them anywhere!' (C. A. Fox.)

It was not long before I knew God's plan. I was being led out by unexpected ways as God's path opened up before me!

One afternoon as I was about to leave the office, one of my co-secretaries, Jean, who knew of my friendship with Gladys, suddenly said 'Oh, I must tell you. I've heard that your friend, Gladys Aylward, is to be on "This is Your Life" this evening!'

I replied doubtfully, 'Are you sure? It's supposed to be a secret, isn't it? I'd have thought Gladys would have written to tell me if she were coming back to Britain.'

Even so, I decided when I got home, that there would be no harm in making sure there was no truth in it, and switched on the TV 'just in case', to discover that Gladys was indeed the subject of 'This is Your Life'. I was so excited I could hardly sit still!

I sent Gladys a greetings telegram and, a few days after the programme, I telephoned some friends in London where I thought she might be staying. Sure enough, she came to the phone.

I asked how she was. 'Fine.'

'And how are your letters, Gladys?' I went on.

'Terrible – I've got nearly a case full,' she said. 'As a matter of fact, Vera, I've locked it up and thrown it into a wardrobe and closed the door. I know I can't possibly reply to them all.'

How I chuckled! This was typical of Gladys! No amount of fame would alter her. It was all right writing a few letters to friends now and then, but a case full – no thank you. Better forget about them.

However, realising how important these letters might be, I suggested that we meet so that I could deal with them, just as I had done on her previous stay in Britain. There and then we arranged a date for her to travel north and I took the following Wednesday off work to meet her at Crewe station.

On my way to the station in my second-hand car, my mind was working overtime. Was this the faint glimmer of light that I had been looking for? Life would be dull no longer with Gladys on the scene! In my wildest dreams I could never have imagined what this was to lead to and the adventures and problems we were to face together.

The train was just coming in! I waited in the middle of the platform, scanning the windows for any sign of Gladys and Gordon, the baby whom she had personally adopted and who had appeared a few days earlier with her on 'This is Your Life'.

Suddenly I caught a glimpse of her. She was trailing up the platform with a suitcase almost as big as herself, and dragging, with great difficulty, a push chair in which sat a black-haired, bright-eyed Chinese boy about fifteen months old.

I raced down the platform to meet her and gave her a big hug. Questions tumbled out as we chatted merrily. I took the case and left Gladys with the push chair, not wanting to scare the baby by paying too much attention to him.

'Say hello to Auntie Vera, Gordon,' said Gladys, pitching her voice a little higher as she always did when she was excited. Gordon just stared, not sure that he wanted any more aunties just yet. He had been surrounded by aunts, uncles and cousins by the dozen since he came to this strange new land and they had all tried to make a fuss of him.

The case containing the stacks of letters was safely stored in the boot and, when Gladys and Gordon were settled in the car, away we went to a friend's house in Poynton, for my mother was not well at that time, and I felt that my sister had more than enough to cope with.

There would be plenty of time later for Gladys to renew the friendship she had made with my family when I was working in the Lake District.

Mary and her husband had offered to put up Gladys and Gordon for the night and to see them on their way the next morning. First it was elevenses. Coffee for the grown-ups and milk and biscuits and a quick change of nappy for our bewildered Gordon, who was then whisked off to have a rest in the cot which friends had provided.

And so at last we tackled that suitcase. Gladys had remembered to bring the key. What a pile of letters – where did we begin? With a short break for lunch, we worked till tea time, opening letters, reading them and trying to sort them into four piles for reply.

Some people had written to ask if Gladys could speak at public meetings or schools; many (including old age pensioners) had sent gifts for the children; while others said how much they had enjoyed the TV programme, or asked whether they could adopt a baby like the one they saw on TV.

When the last letter was opened and in its appropriate pile, we carefully packed them into the suitcase again and decided that we could make time for tea. After that, I knew I must think of leaving. Having stowed that suitcase carefully in the boot again, and said farewell to Gladys and my friends, I headed home, where mother, Lilian and George were agog to hear what that suitcase really had contained!

Back at work the next morning, my colleagues were also intrigued. Lyn and Mary, two of my secretarial friends, immediately offered to help me with the letters. Each evening after work, we would begin on Gladys's work, and not just a suitcase either. Letters continued to roll in as Gladys sent on her correspondence to us. We worked day and night and still they came! It was quite a problem keeping up and I asked God to show me how to

17

cope with this mounting responsibility, in view of the fact that I had a full-time job. I was having to book up speaking engagements for her, too. When she was asked to three or four different engagements in the same town on the same evening, she just said, 'Pass the letters on to Vera.'

Gradually the realisation came that Gladys needed a full-time helper. As I prayed about this, I knew that I was the one to join her. But would she see it the same way?

'Gladys,' I said when I next met her, 'I feel that you really need someone to help you full time. I'm perfectly happy to leave the university and join you if you feel that this is what God wants us to do.'

'Quite honestly, Vera, I do,' she replied without hesitation, and that was that. It never entered my head to ask how much holiday I would get, how much I would be paid for the job, or how many hours a day I would be expected to work. This was God's plan for my life, and I knew it as surely as if a voice had boomed forth from Heaven.

The next step was to tell my boss at the university and cancel my holiday. The arrangements had been made months earlier with a friend and the holiday was due in only a couple of weeks.

As a result of a quick phone call, however, I discovered that to cancel a continental holiday at such short notice, left me liable for the full fee! I didn't want to let my friend down either, so I decided to go.

After my holiday in July, I would leave the university office at the end of August and join Gladys in September.

3
Swiss interlude

The house party to which my friend, Marina, and I were going, was in the Bernese Oberland, at a tiny place called Muerren. Tom and Jean Rees, who ran the holiday centre at Hildenborough Hall, had booked a hotel there for six weeks for three house parties, each of two weeks' duration. They had also booked the Swiss chef. The hotel staff, however, were a different matter. Tom and Jean had invited fifty students to go to Switzerland with them to run the hotel. Two weeks before the house parties were due to begin, the students had a crash course on the arts of being a waitress, a chambermaid, a hostess and all the other work that running a hotel entails.

At last, after travelling by boat and train from England, a crowd of eager guests climbed in the funicular railway train to the tiny village of Muerren perched part way up the mountain. The view on arrival was breathtaking! The hotel looked very grand and just to the left were the beautiful towering peaks of Moench, Eiger and Jungfrau. As far as the eye could see, Swiss chalets were dotted on the mountainsides – their window boxes a blaze of colour as begonias, geraniums and other colourful blooms enhanced the beauty of the marvellous scenery.

Having unpacked, washed and changed, we went downstairs to meet our fellow guests. Everyone looked strange and shy, but it was not long before we were chatting happily together.

Each evening we met in the lounge for informal talks and discussions and it was inspiring to listen to Eric Alexander or Tom Rees speak and to share in each other's experiences. One evening, Tom Rees asked if I would be willing to tell the guests what I hoped to do when I joined the now famous Gladys Aylward, the following month. I agreed, feeling somewhat nervous because I didn't really know quite what the future held myself. I quickly looked through my Bible, wondering how on earth I would begin. From one of its pages dropped out a slip of paper which had been a help to me a year before. I read again the verse from Jeremiah 29: 11: 'I know the plans which I am planning for you, plans of welfare, and not of calamity, to give you a future and a hope.'

Getting to my feet, I explained that I was hoping to help Miss Aylward with her correspondence, the booking of engagements and anything else necessary. I wasn't really sure what the future held, but I did know Who held the future. Here I quoted my special verse, saying that I knew God would clearly guide in the future as He had done in the past. I described also how I had met Gladys, mentioning that, as she had had so many requests for speaking engagements, we hoped to do a tour of Britain and visit the principal towns.

At the end of the evening, I was approached by one of the members of the house party whom I had got to know a little. He was a teacher from Dundee. Could we possibly visit Scotland? Excellent speakers did not often travel 'north of the Border' as he put it, and with the help of a few friends, he would organise the booking of large halls in Edinburgh, Glasgow, Dundee and Aberdeen, if we could only give him one or two dates. At that time, of course, I could not promise anything, but said we would certainly consider fitting Scotland into Gladys's tour, so he gave me his address.

As Jim and his friend were leaving the house party a

day early to go on to Germany for a few days, he asked whether I would like to join him and a number of friends to have '*kaffee und kuchen*' in a little hotel nearby. I gladly accepted, and when we waved goodbye to Jim I wondered whether I would, in fact, come across him on my future travels with Gladys.

The following day we had an uneventful journey back to Britain and I travelled on to Capernwray Hall to spend two or three days with Gladys there before returning to finish my work at the university. What a joy it was to see her again and to talk of what we felt God wanted us to do when I joined her in a few weeks' time. When we parted I knew that Gladys was due to travel to London to fulfil various speaking engagements. The next time we met, at the end of the month, we should begin our work together.

4
On the road

On the first Monday in September, I travelled to
London to join Gladys. It was a beautiful autumn
day. My heart was full of joy, for although I was taking
a step of faith into the unknown, I was looking forward to the 'plans of welfare' that God had in mind for
me.

The very next day I insisted that Gladys see a solicitor;
I knew her affairs were in quite a muddle and it would be
wise for her to form a 'Gladys Aylward Trust', then all
monies given to her work in the future could go into this
account and be safeguarded. From my training at
business college, I also knew that one had to be extremely
careful when dealing with money received from the
public. My short banking career before joining the staff
of Capernwray Hall proved useful, too. Immediately I
joined Gladys, I started a cash book and kept a strict
account of all money received and any expenses we in-
curred. As far as salary was concerned, however, there
was no regular pattern; I didn't receive a salary for the
first five months. Instead, Gladys would occasionally
hand me a pound note with the words, 'Just in case you
need toothpaste or something, dear.'

But the rewards which I received could not be counted
in monetary terms. Helping Gladys, taking care of
Gordon, typing letters, booking seats on trains – I enjoyed these and all the other hundred and one things
which a good 'Girl Friday' does. In any case, I didn't

need any money. As we moved around the country together, we received wonderful hospitality.

Our first trip took us to Blackpool and Manchester to a nurses' prize-giving at which Gladys spoke. How they loved her! She was presented with a beautiful bouquet and a gift for her work. Then at the end of the first week, we went over to Northern Ireland for a fortnight and on to Dublin for two engagements before travelling by air to Scotland to visit Jim's school and take engagements in other Scottish towns.

After my Swiss holiday, when Jim had asked me to persuade Gladys to travel 'north of the Border' if she possibly could, I had discovered that we could in fact travel to Scotland from Dublin. So I had suggested that we offer Jim five days, on the understanding that, to save too much travelling, we do Glasgow, Edinburgh, Dundee and Aberdeen in that order. Jim soon found people eager to help in the organising of four large meetings. Gladys was booked to speak at the Tent Hall, Glasgow, the Usher Hall, Edinburgh, the Caird Hall, Dundee and in a large church in Aberdeen. We knew from experience that so many people wanted to hear her that it was no use booking a small hall! The most vivid example had been Leicester in July. She had originally been booked to speak in a small chapel. I had had to use all my powers of persuasion to get the kind lady who had arranged the meeting to cancel this and to book the large De Montford Hall.

'But how can we possibly pay for such a place?' she asked.

I told her I was sure God would provide the money either through her, through us or through someone else. The collection at that meeting was about £500, and a local business man said, 'Don't take anything off for the hire of the hall. I'll pay for it.'

God is not a pauper and this was demonstrated in a

23

very practical way time and time again as we travelled the country. On our way to Northern Ireland by boat, Gladys and I put Gordon in his push-chair while we collected our cases ready to land. We only moved a few yards away to pick up the luggage, but in that short spell of time we discovered that Gordon's hands were full of bank notes! Someone had recognised the 'Small Woman' and her 'son', and had waited for the chance to give her something without being seen.

We were certainly meeting well-wishers everywhere – in schools, on trains, in shops or at sea. Wherever we went, people recognised Gladys and her equally important small charge.

Everywhere we went, too, there were queues of people trying to get into the large halls which had been booked. Even when the halls were full, people still queued, as if by some miracle the walls of the building could be made to bulge out a little, making room for just a few more!

How very different it was from those early days when she had first gone out to mainland China. To get an audience then was almost impossible. The local people in Yangcheng looked upon her and Jeannie Lawson, with whom Gladys worked, as 'foreign devils'. Nothing daunted, however, and sure that God had sent them to introduce Jesus Christ to the Chinese, Gladys and Jeannie decided that they might have more success with the mule-trains which came through the gates of the city to find lodging at the local inns. They hit on a brilliant idea: they would, themselves, open an inn! Once the muleteers were inside, Jeannie could tell them stories from the Bible. The only trouble was that when the inn was officially opened, no-one dared to enter. It fell to Gladys's lot to leap on to the head of the first mule and to drag the frightened beast into the courtyard of the inn! Gladys, equally terrified, hung on for dear life and the other six animals, tethered to the leading one, had no option but to follow. The muleteer, scared to death, crept fearfully in behind, since he had no wish to lose his beasts. Jeannie and Gladys were delighted: an audience of one was better than none at all.

As we faced capacity crowds in Northern Ireland, those early days when an audience of one was a great catch, were a long way behind. News of our arrival soon spread to the press. Belfast reporters arrived one morning while we were still having breakfast. Gladys was quite prepared for them to take her picture feeding one of her 'children', and Gordon obliged by eating up his banana and smiling at the photographer.

Two days later there was to be a repeat of the 'This is Your Life' programme, on an evening when Gladys had a speaking engagement. The odds were that she would speak for her 'normal' time – anything from one to two hours – and usually the audience did not mind. But not on this occasion! 'Could Gladys possibly speak for a shorter time this evening so that we can see the programme?'

The request was passed on to her, but she was not too pleased. 'They've all seen the programme once, haven't they?' she said, raising her voice excitedly. 'Why on earth do they want to see it again?'

I tried to explain that it would be good to co-operate as they were obviously so thrilled that she had been on television. Then a further suggestion was made – the preliminaries could be cut down to give her more time, and she finally agreed!

But on the night I wondered – *could* she finish on time? For time meant nothing to her when she was speaking. I sat 'on pins' as the time drew near for her to end ... then heaved a great sigh of relief. She *was* finishing. There were smiles all round the audience! She announced the last hymn and as soon as the benediction had been said, people hurriedly made for the door. The hall emptied in a matter of minutes, as if a whirlwind had hit it. I looked at Gladys and she looked at me, not knowing what to make of it. Usually folk lingered, vying with each other to have a word with her. Gladys couldn't for the life of her understand what had got into these people, and she sat on. Eventually I went over and whispered to her, 'Come on Gladys. We're going round to Mrs. Brown's house to watch your programme. They're waiting for us!'

'Hmp!' was her disgruntled reply, as if to say 'Why does anybody want to see *that* again?' She came, nevertheless, and was as quiet as a mouse while we sat and enjoyed the repeat of 'This is Your Life'.

There was such enthusiasm about the programme afterwards that she thawed out and began to talk. The room was filled with neighbours who had been thrilled to watch the television with the subject of the programme sitting in the same room. Now they wanted to talk to her.

In Northern Ireland, although based with some friends of Gladys's in Belfast, we travelled to various towns, often with a school meeting in the afternoon and a public meeting in the evening. We usually tried to take Gordon with us to the former, as the children loved meeting him. They would offer him little gifts and try to feed him with crisps and other things. It was no wonder that he grew into a fat bouncy toddler!

If the evening meeting was near to our base, Gordon would accompany us and after ten minutes or so, I would creep out with him to put him to bed. Our audience loved seeing the 'baby' at these meetings, but I had my own views on his bedtime. In any case, if he was allowed to sit on the platform with Gladys, I was at my wits' end trying to keep him quiet while she was speaking.

On one dreadful occasion some well-meaning friend had given him a tube of sweets right at the beginning of the meeting. I spent the rest of the evening surreptitiously trying to retrieve them from the floor and handing them to him, only to find that they had been thrown down again immediately! It was a good game while it lasted, but the strain was too much for me. After all, the audience had come to hear Gladys, not to watch the antics of one small boy, however amusing he might be.

5
North of the border

Our two weeks in Northern Ireland passed all too quickly and we were soon travelling across to Scotland, where an equally warm welcome awaited us from the Scots.

From the Tent Hall, Glasgow, we moved to Edinburgh. The Usher Hall was so packed that many people could not get in. At the start there were still crowds of folk outside. It seemed such a pity, so I decided to take Gordon outside to talk to a few folk. If they were not able to see Gladys, then I wanted to make sure that they did see her adopted son.

At the sight of us, everyone's face lit up! Of course, they recognised Gordon from the TV programme, for he had on his small black Chinese skull cap and long padded embroidered Chinese coat. As I moved along the queue chatting and getting Gordon to say 'Hello' (one of his few English words), the crowd were delighted.

All too soon we had to return to the inside of the hall. You could have heard a pin drop! Every eye was on the tiny figure, with a large Bible raised in her right hand as she told of her friendship with the Almighty. *He* had brought her through unforgettable experiences, *He* had spoken to her, showing her which pathways to take, *He* had delivered her that she might speak for Him in the land of her birth. At almost all her meetings there was one clarion call.

'People of Britain,' she would say in her clear, ringing voice, 'Turn to the Almighty God. Turn to His Son Jesus

Christ before Communism takes over your land. And don't tell me that it can't! We never thought it could happen in China, but it did. Wake up, before it is too late!'

To Gladys the issue was clear cut. It was Communism or Christ. Many of us who listened to her then were not sure at that time that Communism *was* a threat to us in peaceful Britain. Wasn't she exaggerating? Maybe we know now that she wasn't. We have been warned by that great man Solzhenitsyn – who knows only too well the terrors of Communism from the inside. How we should thank God for our freedom and never cease to serve Him.

Many people accepted the challenge to faith in Christ as Gladys spoke. Today, they and countless others know the peace and joy of God in their everyday lives.

From Edinburgh we went to Aberdeen and then on to Dundee, finishing our small Scottish tour there. We had two evenings in that area and the Caird Hall had been booked for the first, while that afternoon, Gladys spoke in the large local school where Jim was teaching and had arranged the meeting. What a welcome we received! The whole school had been assembled and the youngsters listened in awe. Many of them wished, I am sure, that they could at that very moment board a boat for China. It would certainly be much more exciting than trying to learn French and German.

News flashed around that Gladys was to be in Dundee for a second night and we received a hasty telephone call: Could Gladys please speak in Perth? They had a hall available. Gladys's response was immediate. 'Yes, of course I can.'

As we came out of the Caird Hall that first evening, Jim was waiting for us. He, too, knew that we had an extra night in Dundee, so now came his request.

'Would you like to spend an evening with me, Vera, and see the slides I took of our Swiss holiday?'

29

I hesitated, knowing that the other speaking engagement had been hurriedly booked, and we should be in Perth the next evening. Gladys immediately came to the rescue. 'Yes, you go my dear,' she said. 'I can easily go to Perth on my own. In any case, friends will be taking me by car. It will be much better if you put Gordon to bed a bit earlier, then go around to Jim's place and see his pictures. It will do you good to have a night off!'

The next day, after tea, my Chinese charge was put to bed slightly earlier than usual. I was looking forward to a most pleasant evening, and was not disappointed. We relived our Swiss holiday as we saw slides and recognised this one and that, and laughed and chatted like two magpies. It was great fun being in the company of this charming Scot.

About 10.30 p.m. I said I must leave to check that Gordon *was* still fast asleep in bed. Jim offered to walk back with me to the house where we were staying. As we parted on the doorstep, Jim asked, 'Would you mind if I write to you sometimes?'

'I don't mind in the least,' I said. 'It would be very nice to hear from you.' I gave him our address, thanked him for a lovely evening and went inside wondering whether I would ever see him again.

Our next port of call was Nottingham. We had a number of school meetings arranged there and a large rally in the Albert Hall. At each place we had a royal reception, Gladys being nearly mobbed at one school by eager youngsters anxious to have a word with her or with Gordon. Bouquets of flowers were lavished on her, dozens of photographs taken for the school records and there were autograph books galore to sign. Gladys loved it all! At the Albert Hall rally she spoke to many people at the end of the meeting. Little did we know then that one lady, Kathleen Langton Smith, was to come into our lives again at a time when we needed her most.

Meanwhile letters were still pouring in. On our travels I found it very difficult to keep up with them, so when two secretaries in Cardiff wrote and asked if they could help us to type any letters, we saw this as a wonderful provision. Gladys and I decided that if these girls helped with the letters, then she and I could travel to Scotland to stay with friends just outside Inverness and there produce a small magazine giving news of her work. At the same time we would send batches of letters on to our Cardiff friends.

Obviously the magazine would take some preparation and we made careful plans. I suggested that we ask for news from Michael, the man who was in charge of the work in Hong Kong, and news of the Home in Formosa. Then Gladys, of course, would write something and I would put in a little report too.

In fact, Michael had been publishing news from time to time in a leaflet called 'Good Hope'. I suggested that we keep the same name for our little magazine and Gladys readily agreed.

We got in touch with our friends near Inverness and accepted their invitation, but, before returning to Scotland, Gladys went to Birmingham to see her brother, and I went home for a few days, armed, of course, with the latest consignment of letters.

Our little office was now being run from the lounge of my minister's small semi-detached home. David and Daphne had willingly given up the use of their sitting-room so that we could litter it with letters, typewriters and all the paraphernalia we needed to keep the work going. They received letters on our behalf and posted them on to us.

Meantime, I had asked our London solicitor to draw up a Charitable Deed of Trust for Gladys. She asked me to be a Trustee, and also Ian Thomas from Capernwray Hall, because he and his wife had been such a tower of strength to her on her previous stay in Britain. We were told by the solicitors that the minimum number of trustees required was three, so we prayed that God would guide us to the third person. Not long afterwards Gladys approached a business man she knew very well in the south of England and he promised to think about it.

In a few days Gladys returned from Birmingham with Gordon, and we prepared to travel to the Highlands. As well as getting our little magazine printed, we intended to catch up on correspondence, so that Gladys could return home to the Far East with the knowledge that she was more or less up to date.

The idea was that when Gladys left Britain, I should run the British Trust office, receive gifts on her behalf and the bank would send them on to her – maintaining the interest in her work which had snowballed as a result of all the publicity from the book *The Small Woman*, the film 'The Inn of the Sixth Happiness' and the TV programmes.

Then a new idea changed all that. We were about to leave home for Scotland, when Gladys suddenly said, 'Vera, don't you think it would be a good idea for you to come out to Taiwan to see the work first?'

The suggestion stunned me!

'But how can I?' I stammered. 'Who would deal with all the work at this end?'

'I'm not sure,' she said, 'but I've got a feeling that you ought to come back to the Far East with me. Things seem in a muddle out there. I could do with you to help me sort them out.'

To her it all seemed so simple, but I could see obstacles at every turn of the way!

'Well, I suppose we could think about it and ask God to show us,' I said, and we left it like that while we journeyed north again to the Scottish Highlands.

It was such a change not to be rushing for trains,

having a meal in one house, then hurrying to the place where Gladys was due to speak, then sleeping in a different bed almost every few nights. It was bliss to settle in one bed in the quiet of the country for a few weeks.

Gordon, too, wouldn't have minded staying there for his whole life. The family were so kind, making their huge dining-room available to us. Gladys and I sat at a long oak table, a typewriter at each end as we worked away day after day.

Good Hope was taking shape by this time and I loved cutting out pictures and fitting these to the appropriate articles or reports. For the front cover I obtained permission from David Steen of *Modern Woman* to use one of his photographs which he had taken to accompany an article on Gladys in that magazine.

Then a letter arrived from Jim: As we were back in Scotland, would it be convenient for him to come up to the Highlands to visit us for the weekend? I consulted Gladys.

'Oh, yes, tell him we shall be pleased to see him. I like him,' she stated bluntly.

'So do I,' I thought as I hastened to get a note in the post assuring him that he would be very welcome, after checking that our 'family' could put him up, too. That weekend we had a most enjoyable time. Gordon got to know 'Uncle Jim' and when he left, Gladys told him to come back again if he could, as we would be there for a few more weeks.

He *did* come back, bringing yet another gorgeous box of chocolates. We were being spoiled, but thoroughly enjoying it.

We had to keep our mind on our work, though. We had not heard from the friend who had been approached about being the third trustee, and time was moving on. It was almost the end of November. We were due to meet the solicitor in London very soon, and our flights to the

Far East had been booked for 15th December, if I was definitely going.

Our time in the Highlands flew by, especially as Gladys had fitted in a few speaking engagements. In fact, one unforgettable day, we had the privilege of visiting Gordonstoun (when Prince Charles was at the school). Gladys spoke to all the boys and they listened eagerly to this dynamic little woman.

Jim had agreed to take care of the financial side of the work while I was away and Gladys asked that he become trustee number three.

Things were beginning to fit into place, enabling me to leave the work in Britain for about two months with an easy conscience. Jim had Ian Thomas to consult with at any time as co-trustee. Meanwhile our two Cardiff secretaries would cope with the correspondence.

We said 'Goodbye' to Jim and Scotland, secure in the knowledge that the right man was holding the fort for us there. We decided to call in at Cardiff on our way down to London, too, so that we could meet 'our secretaries'. Mair and Joan were most efficient and we knew that they would cope beautifully with 'those letters' during my absence.

Then a few days were spent in London tying up the Gladys Aylward Trust, and including a trip to Benenden School where Gladys spoke to all the girls, Princess Anne being in the audience.

The day afterwards, I sped home again full of excitement, thinking of all I had to pack for my two month trip to the Far East.

We were to fly out to Hong Kong on 15th December and then on to Taiwan just before or after Christmas. The thought of Christmas in the East thrilled me! What *would* it be like?

6
Hong Kong

My family were marvellous as they helped me get ready for this exciting chapter in my life. They all recognised that I was going on a God-directed mission.

I dug out the one or two cotton dresses in my possession and bought a few items of cotton underwear, having been advised not to take nylon to wear in the heat of the Far East. But my mind was in a whirl. What else did I need? Gladys had given me some tips on what to take and what not to take – but as we were going by air, the amount of luggage we were allowed was naturally limited. Oh, yes, I thought, I must take some ointment just in case I got mosquito bites. Little did I know!

During the last few weeks I had various injections which almost knocked me out, particularly the one for typhus. I was sure they had given me the disease by mistake and that I would never recover. Survive I did, however.

At last I was ready with my new green case, a parting gift from the university, packed. I got the morning train south from Crewe, where my family waved 'Goodbye'. I had promised to let them have news as soon as humanly possible on my arrival in the East. But first, I was to spend three days in London with Gladys so that we could make sure all our business affairs were straight.

In London we had barely unpacked for our brief stay, when we had a last minute telephone call from the BBC.

Could Miss Aylward possibly do six talks for the 'Lift Up Your Hearts' programme for next week?

I had answered the telephone and told Gladys about the request.

'No, they are far too late,' was her reply. 'I couldn't possibly do them in a couple of days. They each have to fit into exactly five minutes. How can I, when we are off to the East on Sunday?'

I thought quickly. It was a pity to miss such a marvellous opportunity. Turning to Gladys I said: 'Do say yes, Gladys, and I will help you. It's such a wonderful chance for you to talk about God on the radio. Who knows how many people will be listening?'

She rose to the challenge as always. 'All right, say "Yes" then, if you think we can.'

Straight away I got out the small portable tape recorder that we were taking out East with us and set up the microphone.

'Now Gladys,' I coaxed, 'just talk to me and tell me a story and I will record it. Why not start with one about Ninepence?'

She obeyed like a lamb, and when the story had been recorded, I typed it out so that she could read it easily. Then I borrowed a watch with a second hand and asked her to read the script back to me. If it was too long, I helped her chop a bit out – if it was too short, then I helped her add a bit. In this way, over the next two days, I recorded six stories, typed them, listened to them and chopped or lengthened them until at long last they were ready. On the Saturday morning, Gladys went to the BBC studio and recorded them. Jim promised to record the broadcasts because the next day, Sunday, we flew off to the Far East, before the stories began to come over the air. I looked forward to listening to them on my return in a month or two. But before then, I was to face the biggest adventure and challenge of my whole life.

Baroness Mary Stocks had kindly offered us a lift to the airport, and when the Land-Rover arrived, with Baroness Stocks driving, we were all packed in – Gladys, Gordon, myself, our cases *and* fourteen parcels of toys which had been given to us for the children in Formosa. We had wondered how we were to get the parcels out there, but, thanks to the intervention of a retired air commodore who approached the air line, they were flown out entirely free.

We arrived at the airport in good time. Gordon was thrilled to see the planes and there was such a hustle and bustle that excitement rose within me also. There is a thrill about travelling by air, catching a glimpse of fellow travellers from all over the world. Willing stewards soon relieved us of the parcels of toys, and we thanked Baroness Stocks for bringing us and said 'Goodbye' to her.

Then we boarded the plane, which was due to leave at 10.15 a.m. We were comfortably settled aboard and two air hostesses checked that everyone was happy. I had never flown in my life until I met Gladys. I was so excited that I didn't want to miss a thing. We had flown briefly before so that we could fit in as many speaking engagements as possible, but I never dreamt that I would ever have the opportunity of flying to the other side of the world.

The route map and flight information looked most intriguing. I browsed through it noticing that the information was given in a number of languages, Chinese included. How complicated it looked. I wondered Gladys ever learnt to speak it.

At last the stewardess announced that we were to fasten our safety-belts, the pilot began to rev up the engines, there was a deafening noise and the plane began to roll down the runway.

We were on our way – Zurich, Rome, Beirut, Karachi, Calcutta, Bangkok and Hong Kong. On the first leg of our journey I wrote a hasty note home so that we could post it in Rome when we got off the plane to look around the airport building.

Believe it or not, at Beirut Airport when we got off the plane again to stretch our legs, someone recognised Gladys! Suddenly a young man, who appeared to be Lebanese, rushed across, produced his autograph book and, with a big smile, made Gladys understand that he wanted her to sign it. She willingly obliged and away he went.

At Karachi we didn't bother to stir ourselves. We had been travelling almost exactly twelve hours, so were feeling rather tired. During the journey the pilot kept us informed of international times, so according to Greenwich Mean Time it was 10.30 p.m. – according to Karachi time it was 3.30 a.m. It was a most odd feeling.

At Calcutta we decided we needed a little exercise. It was 2.20 a.m. GMT but our watches told us that it was 7.50 a.m. I was struck by the obvious poverty at Calcutta airport. Thin looking, sad-eyed dogs wandered all over the place. Everything looked shabby and I thought of the hungry multitudes in that country and of the wonderful work being done by Mother Teresa, in that very city.

On the way to Bangkok we had breakfast at 3 a.m. GMT and it seemed quite out of keeping to have lunch at 7 a.m. GMT. We did not leave the plane at Bangkok as we were trying to get a little more sleep. How could one sleep on such an exciting journey? And, of course, there was the crying of the very youngest passengers, some of whom were only a few months old.

Gordon, however, was very good and we tried to amuse him by showing him little picture books for he could now say quite a few words and understood much more.

Gladys talked to him about my presence as well, 'Isn't it nice to have Auntie Vera with us Gordon?' she said, raising her voice as she usually did when speaking to him. 'We're taking her home to show her where we live.'

Gordon just smiled at us both. It was good to have two women looking after him. What more could a young man wish!

The plane at last touched down at Kai Tak airport, Kowloon. It had been a very long journey and, although tired, I had not wanted to miss a minute. Hong Kong greeted us with friendly warmth. To my amazement, a reception committee awaited us as we walked down the steps of the plane. A garland of paper flowers was placed around Gladys's neck and a similar one around mine. Then a huge bouquet of roses was handed to Gladys and an equally large bouquet of gladioli to me. These friends were from the Chinese church.

Everyone began chattering away in Chinese, faces beaming. They each bowed low as Gladys introduced them to me. Gordon and I were bewildered! Half a dozen reporters surged around Gladys for a story, cameras lifted as they vied with each other for the best picture and there was general pandemonium.

We came out of the airport buildings, found a taxi waiting for us and in no time at all we were on our way to Michael's home in Kowloon, which was a third floor flat in a large block.

On the way, I looked through the taxi window, there seemed to be people everywhere. Colourful Chinese signs decorated the shops on either side of the road and, down alleyways, multitudes of clothes hung from bamboo poles. The place was teeming with life. No wonder! Before the war the population of Hong Kong had been just over a million – it was now over three million. Where did all these people live? I was soon to find out.

Michael's wife, Maureen, we discovered, was away in the United States taking a Bible course and learning English at the same time. Meanwhile their three small children aged from three to seven were taken care of by a Chinese girl who came in daily.

On arrival at Michael's small home, Gladys was given a very tiny room with Gordon. I was also given another tiny room. I discovered later that Michael had squeezed himself into one room with his three children so as to make us as comfortable as possible. How hospitable Chinese families are! We spent only ten days there before flying on to Taiwan, but they still stand out in my memory.

Tourists do not normally include refugee settlements in their holiday tour, but I was no tourist and wanted to see for myself how people on the other side of the world lived. I was also trying to record, with the aid of my camera, what I saw, so that I could enlighten friends at home.

So, on Christmas Eve, we set out for Chai Wan, the refugee settlement where Gladys had a school. We took the bus through the maze of busy streets and got the ferry-boat across to Hong Kong island. Another bus took us away from all the big hotels, the luxury flats and inviting shops to an area where tiny shacks were scattered all over the hillside alongside huge towering blocks.

When we got off the bus, it was all bare-looking and uninviting. Michael led the way past building after building. Finally we entered one. Inside, it was stifling hot, the smell almost unbearable, and my head reeled with the screeching noise of hundreds of children playing outside and inside. Their cries seemed to echo and re-echo from building to building around the whole area as we started up the stairs to the roof. How did people put up with it all, I wondered. How did they stand the heat? I soon realised that they had no option.

We climbed round and round, up stair after stair, to the very top. I was concerned for Gladys and asked 'Are you all right?'

'Oh, yes, I'm all right, dear,' she replied. 'I'm used to this.'

How many other women, over sixty years of age, would have tackled those stairs with such gusto? Most would have preferred to close their eyes to all the human need and tragedy so apparent amongst those refugees. Not so, Gladys! She revelled in helping folk less fortunate than herself.

When we reached the rooftop, we discovered a school in progress. Swarms of children came to greet us. We passed through roughly made classrooms strung out along the roof, to reach the playground end where we were to have our Christmas celebrations. I was relieved to see strong wire fences, interspersed with tough iron bars, enclosing the rooftop so that there was no chance of any child falling off!

Very soon our Christmas party was in full swing. We forgot the bareness of the scene as tiny tots acted out nativity plays and others sang, eagerly awaiting their turn to jump on to the wobbly platform to do their party piece. They were adorable!

At the end of the proceedings each child was handed some nuts and sweets and an orange and off they went, hurrying to join the rest of their family, either in a nearby shack or the one room which they called home in one of the huge re-settlement blocks of flats.

Each family, whatever the size, had to live, eat and sleep in that one room or shack. One Canadian reporter visiting the island said that a Canadian dog had more room than a Chinese family living in the shacks on the hillsides of Hong Kong!

After the party, we visited one such shack for ourselves. Three middle-aged Chinese women were living in conditions which were really indescribable, their pathetic pile of belongings crowded into a corner, to be brought out and made up into beds when we had gone. One of the women was responsible for cleaning the rooftop school-rooms. She felt it was a privilege to do this work for God – and for Gladys. She had a joy in her heart which many women all over the world never find, even with washing machines, fridges and all the other mod cons. We gave her some knitted blankets which had been sent out by Queenie, Gladys's cousin, for just such a need as this. Queenie had faithfully backed up Gladys in her work for many years and spent day after day sorting out clothes and blankets packed in the garage of a London flat. Rosemary, another special friend of Gladys's, was a tremendous help in this work too, and between the two of them, they had sent out hundreds of parcels to Hong Kong and Taiwan, to gladden the heart of some orphan or refugee family.

At 10.30 p.m. we finally left the settlement to wend our way back to Kowloon and Michael's flat, arriving there completely exhausted, just before midnight. But we had barely staggered into bed before we were awakened, by what sounded like a Salvation Army band! I thought I must be dreaming, but no – there it was again. I looked at my clock. It was two o'clock in the morning; whatever was going on?

A head appeared around my bedroom door.

'Can you get up and join us for a few minutes, Vera?' Gladys asked.

'Yes,' I replied. 'Is something wrong?'

'Oh, no,' she laughed, 'it's Christmas Day and the young people from the Hope Mission have dropped in to wish us a happy Christmas.'

I *must* be dreaming, I thought. But nonetheless I put on a coat and staggered out of the room. A sea of smiling Chinese faces greeted me and my appearance was the signal for trumpets to be lifted and a Christmas carol blared forth. The noise almost raised the roof!

At the end of the carol, they had one request – would I

please sing a carol for them in English now? At this early hour? I thought. Yet how could I refuse? I made a supreme effort and sang out the only one that I could think of – 'O come all ye faithful', feeling neither joyful nor triumphant at that time of the night!

But they were delighted and clapped loudly and, after playing one more roof-raising, ear-splitting carol on the trumpets, they left noisily to go to the next home.

I went back to bed gladly but was rudely awakened a short time later by the noise of buckets clanging, jugs rattling and water gushing from the taps. I looked at my clock again – only 5.30 a.m.! It was not only Christmas Day – it was water day!

I discovered there had been a drought in Hong Kong for nearly a year, and we were allowed water only every four days when the taps were turned on, usually from 6 a.m. to 9 a.m. This particular morning they were turned on early and there was bedlam as every member of the family rushed to the taps with jugs, buckets and containers of every kind to make sure they had sufficient water to last the next four days.

Realising that there was no more sleep to be had, we decided to make the most of the beautiful weather and Gladys suggested we take the four children out for a morning trip up the Peak, the highest point on Hong Kong island. Before long we had them all washed, dressed and fed. Warm hands clung to ours as we wended our way up the Peak, first getting a bus and then the funicular railway. The children gabbled away happily in Chinese, voices rising as we approached journey's end.

Standing at the top of the Peak, Gladys and I feasted our eyes on the lovely views. Gorgeous red poinsettias grew everywhere, the sun shone with penetrating warmth and it seemed the world was a very beautiful place to live in.

But for some the story was very different. I thought of

our visit only the day before to the squalid refugee settlement at Chai Wan and wished with all my heart that they could live in such a lovely place. Did they realise that such a place as the Peak existed? I doubted it somehow.

My attention was drawn away from these thoughts by the children trying to show us the treasures they had found – shiny stones, dainty little flowers, bits of this and that. Michael's children came to accept my sign language, although Thomas, the eldest, felt rather sorry for this somewhat backward grown-up, who couldn't speak a word of his language properly. He patiently tried to communicate with me. When he got frustrated, he turned his attention to Grandma Aylward. Michael was one of Gladys's first 'children' from earlier days on the mainland of China, and Gladys was very proud of her three 'grandchildren'.

We eventually made our way homewards for we were expected at the Hope Mission in Kowloon that afternoon for another Christmas party. The large room at the Mission had been transformed with tables set ready for a feast. Gay decorations hung from the ceilings. Michael, who had left home earlier to ensure that preparations were well in hand, now welcomed us with his beaming smile. Samuel, his colleague, eagerly shook our hands and bowed low. This was the day they had been waiting for. How thrilled they were to have Gladys with them over the Christmas period!

By this time I was beginning to get used to Chinese food. During my first few days in Hong Kong I found it very difficult to be offered rice for breakfast, lunch and tea, with only small variations of food sitting on top. After the first few days, I felt decidedly off colour! I was, however, becoming quite adept in the art of using chopsticks. It was a good thing I had persevered because the food, that day, was most appetising. They had, of course, saved specially for this feast. Normally the everyday diet was poor but adequate.

After the party, Gladys spoke and I was asked to say a few words while she translated for me. Everyone seemed to be enjoying themselves to the full. Then Gladys and I were each presented with a beautiful white brooch. The Chinese characters on hers meant 'Long life', on mine 'Blessings'.

The beauty of a Chinese feast is that no one is in a hurry, so I was not surprised to see from my watch that it was nearing 10 p.m. when Gladys suggested that it was time to go home.

On arrival back at Michael's flat, the home-help informed us that a visitor had been to see us earlier. Her name was Wong Kwai and she had left a message to say that she would return the next day.

I remembered that I had met Wong Kwai in London in the 1950s when she had been staying with Gladys whom she had first met in Belfast. Gladys had heard that a Chinese woman was in a mental home there, so made a point of going to see her. There was very little wrong with Wong Kwai which a loving heart and secure home with Gladys could not put right, and she obtained her discharge and eventually arranged for her to return to her son in Hong Kong. We looked forward to seeing her again.

The next day was spent getting ready for our onward journey to Taiwan. There were clothes to be washed, since we had received fresh water through the taps the previous day, and letters to be done – so that we did not find our correspondence too far behind on arrival in Taiwan. Jim had written assuring us that all was well on the home front and that he was managing to cope with the gifts which had been steadily flowing in for the work since our departure. Mair and Joan also wrote to let us know that their evenings were being spent in dealing with correspondence on our behalf.

Just before lunch, Wong Kwai reappeared with her grandson, anxious to have a few words with Gladys. She was fit and well and, in her own simple way, seeking to show the love of Jesus to her neighbours in the tenements of Hong Kong.

The following day we bade our friends farewell. Quite a crowd gathered at the airport to see us off and to wish us God-speed. An hour later we touched down at Taipei airport in Taiwan.

7
Ilha Formosa – Isle Beautiful

It was far more thrilling to arrive at Taipei than Hong Kong, for this was Gladys's home. *She* could hardly wait to see all her children again, and *I* could hardly imagine what life on Taiwan would be like.

As soon as the plane touched down, we were chatting away exuberantly. 'Come on Gordon, we're home now,' said Gladys in her excited, high pitched voice. 'Auntie Vera is going to meet all the rest of the family ... I'll carry Gordon, dear, if you bring our bags,' she added turning to me.

She headed for the exit. As she began to descend the steps of the plane, one of her family rushed halfway up and placed a garland of paper flowers around her neck. When I followed her, another garland was placed around mine. High ranking officers of the air force, army and navy were there to greet us, as well as Madame Chiang Kai-Shek's deputy. Hordes of other friends crowded around Gladys and Gordon, whilst anxious photographers tried their best to wriggle through to take pictures for the newspapers. It was not surprising. The Small Woman was world famous and the Taiwanese were more than proud of their friend and fellow citizen.

At last the reporters won and, after all the official greetings and bows and handshakes, they managed to persuade Gladys to give them an interview, which lasted three quarters of an hour. We all had to sit patiently, until they had finished.

As I couldn't speak a word of Chinese, I whiled away the time browsing through the booklets which enlightened tourists on the way of life of the island and its people. From the air, the island appeared rather drab so I was surprised to read in a booklet that its original name was '*Ilha Formosa*' meaning 'Isle Beautiful'. Portuguese sailors who chanced upon the place four hundred years ago, had given it this name and, as I was to discover later, the name was well deserved.

At last the reporters were satisfied and we were taken by taxi to Gladys's humble home. The journey for me was terrifying! For one thing, there was the constant noise of car horns blowing continuously as streams of traffic – cars, pedicabs, bicycles, buffalo or ox carts – sought to go in the direction that *they* wanted. For another, there seemed to be no rule of the road. One minute we were on the left, the next on the right, depending on the taxi driver's expertise.

As in Hong Kong, gay and colourful signs hung outside various shops and there was an air of excitement known only to the East. On one or two inevitable stops to avoid an accident, I could watch customer and shopkeeper bargaining about the sale of some article with each other, on the pavement – an experience yet in store for me.

Eventually the traffic began to thin out as we came to the outskirts of the town. Grey-roofed houses and flats took the place of shops. We turned down a road past a muddy little river, round the corner and down a lane, and at last arrived at Gladys's house.

The tiny living-room, with its brick-tiled floor, was full of eager friends who were delighted at Gladys's homecoming. We were soon sitting down while willing hands pressed us to have a cup of milkless China tea which had small white flowers in it. I sipped it and, although not particularly appreciating the taste, I gladly drank it up because I was thirsty.

Esther Huang, one of Gladys's best friends, was seeing to our refreshments. She had one of the most beautiful faces I have ever seen. Although she knew hardly any English, she shook my hand warmly, beamed upon me and assured me in her own way that I was more than welcome.

Two of the people who had met us at the airport were the Superintendent of the Children's Home and his wife; the latter had been adopted by Gladys some years ago when she was a child on the mainland of China. She had married in Tiawan and now she and her husband ran the Children's Home at Peitou, where they spent most of their time. But they also had a house next door to Gladys for their own family of three.

At last the friends left and we began to unpack Gladys's things, which had been stowed away in the superintendent's house next door, in case of thieves. They had visited Gladys's house on a previous occasion when she was abroad, so she took no chances now.

We made up Gladys's bed next, with a sheet and a thin type of quilt, and found sufficient small blankets for the cot in Gladys's room for Gordon. We then looked around for something for my bed in the next room. There was nothing; yet we were sure the couple in charge of the Home knew that I was returning with Gladys. Why hadn't they bought some extra bedding for the spare bed?

Gladys seemed surprised. 'Never mind, Vera,' she said, as we looked around the completely bare room. 'Suppose you have those lovely knitted blankets which we brought back with us from England, just for one night? Tomorrow I'll go out and buy something for your bed.'

The blankets in question had been made from bits of colourful wool knitted into squares and sewn together.

The only snag was that most of them were intended for babies' cots! I managed, however, with about half a dozen small ones and one larger one, which could be used as a quilt. I lay on a large towel which Gladys produced and she draped the blankets over me. For a pillow I used clothes out of my case.

The fact that I then spent an uncomfortable night was not only due to the lack of bedding, but also due to the presence of large brown cockroaches in my bedroom! Gladys had rigged up a small lamp for me and when I found I couldn't sleep, I switched on the light. I lay stiff with horror as I saw dozens of these horrible creatures scurrying away across the floor. Whatever would happen if they crawled into the bed? I asked myself. Ugh!

Very thankfully I welcomed the dawn and got up, and went through to the tiny little bathroom, which to Gladys was a real luxury, in spite of the fact that the lavatory was more often than not out of action!

Soon the house was astir. Gladys and Gordon appeared at their bedroom door and Yang So (Gladys's Chinese woman) appeared from a tiny box-room behind the kitchen; if it could be called a kitchen! It was merely a confined space just inside the back door, where all the cooking was done on a brick-built contraption, a huge cylinder of calor gas providing the necessary heating. All the food was fried in a big black frying pan, with the exception of the rice which was boiled in another pan. Here, too, the water was heated and carried to the bathroom, if one wanted a wash, for there were no hot water taps for it to run through. It was considered a real luxury to have a bath to stand in while you washed with a pan of hot water from the kitchen.

Later we had our breakfast in the very small dining-room, situated just beside the kitchen. It contained a table, four chairs and a cupboard for food. There wasn't room for anything more.

As I was still finding it difficult to get used to Chinese food and Gordon had been feeling the same way, we had an English breakfast of bread, margarine, marmalade and coffee. We had brought the coffee and marmalade with us to Taiwan for this purpose. Gordon had to have powdered milk because it was not possible to buy fresh milk on the island.

After breakfast we quickly went shopping for some essentials – like bedding! Gladys also bought a small teapot, a kettle and a tiny little electric ring for me to use in my bedroom, because she knew that I had brought from home one precious packet of Ceylon tea, and wanted me to indulge in the luxury of a cup if I felt off colour.

We hurried home with our purchases, for we had been invited to a special welcome luncheon in town, laid on in Gladys's honour by various women's committees, and several women representatives from the Senate would be there.

The official luncheon was held in a big women's club, and about forty or fifty women were present. Gladys sat with Gordon at the head of the table, surrounded by well-known Taiwanese officials – Madame Chiang Kai-Shek's deputy, Madame's personal chaplain and many others. But I crept in at the back with Barbara, a British friend of Gladys's.

Barbara was visiting us from Puli hospital where she was the matron. When she had first come out to Taiwan some years before, as a result of hearing Gladys preach in Canada, she had helped Gladys for a brief time and then gone down to Puli. She was doing a wonderful job, contacting teenage girls amongst the mountain tribes-people, then bringing them to the hospital and training them as nurses. She had had great success in this difficult and sometimes dangerous task. Now she was having a few days' well-earned rest in Taipei. While we ate the delightful Chinese meal, I was glad to have Barbara to talk to amongst all the chattering in Chinese that was going on around us.

There were various speeches from prominent people, then Gladys rose to speak. At the end of her speech, to my utter astonishment, she called me up to the front and asked me to speak also. I had little option as all eyes were upon me.

Gladys explained that a Chinese lady nearby would interpret for me, so, in simple words, I told the assembled company how I felt that God had given me this work to do, for I had committed my life to Him for His service. I briefly told how I had met Gladys originally and of our hopes for the future. With a great sigh of relief I sat down.

Barbara was staying with a young American missionary couple in Taipei, who kindly invited us to their home for the evening. It made a very pleasant change to eat American food and we all ate heartily. Their home was beautiful and I could not help but compare it with Gladys's bare little dwelling. Americans certainly took care of their missionaries very well. They seemed to be able to give far more freely to missions than we do in Britain. I felt rather ashamed. Were not our missionaries worth just as much loving care? I felt even more determined to do all I could for Gladys.

When we got back to Gladys's home, we were delighted to find one or two Christmas cards from Britain awaiting us. One delightful card from a lady in Stoke-on-Trent, was simply addressed to:

'Miss Gladys Aylward, Missionary somewhere in
Formosa and
Miss Porter, her secretary.
(The Inn of the Sixth Happiness)'

It had found us, nevertheless, and all the greetings brought joy to our hearts.

Then we simply *had* to get Gordon, now known by his Chinese name of Chi Kuang, to bed, for it was well past his normal bedtime and he was half asleep already. In no time at all he was safely tucked up in the cot in Gladys's room and Gladys and I sat down to chat in her tiny living-room. It seemed as if I had been in the Far East for months. I had, in fact, been in Hong Kong for precisely ten days and in Taiwan for barely two!

I did not relish the thought of going to bed because of those awful cockroaches, which even dared to come out of their hideouts during the day! When this happened Gladys would calmly whip off her slipper and with quick deft movements slay the creatures. How could I, therefore, express my horror at the nocturnal habits of these huge beetle-like insects? We said good night and I crept into my room. I was very honest with God as I had my usual chat with Him before going to sleep. I told Him that I appreciated all His help on this day of unexpected opportunities to speak for Him. I thanked Him for the privilege of being in His service and of helping Gladys and all the children, but I added one heartfelt prayer as I closed: 'Dear Lord, I don't know how long I can stick sleeping in this room with these awful creepy crawlies!'

After a fitful night's sleep, I got up, feeling nevertheless excited because we were to go up to the Children's Home at Peitou to celebrate Christmas belatedly with them. I was looking forward to this immensely. Gladys and I took a red taxi for the journey because the village of Peitou was situated about twelve miles out of Taipei.

On the way, I leaned forward to see as much as possible through the taxi window. We were soon leaving the grey-roofed houses and flats behind, and were in more open country with paddy-fields on either side of the road. A huge water-buffalo plodded through thick muddy water pulling a rough wooden plough, guided by a man following behind. He, too, was wading in the mess, trousers rolled up beyond his knees.

We were travelling far too fast and I couldn't see all that I wanted. But suddenly we had to slow down behind a bus. This was much better, for I could see an old granny, sitting outside a one-storey long, low building, hens scratching around the earth at her feet in a minute small-holding. One or two children played hide-and-seek whilst granny, legs astride, held out the baby. What better way of toilet-training a youngster! No doubt the parents were already hard at work in the paddy fields, anxious not to lose any precious time before the rainy season.

Eventually we got past the bus and I noticed on the left hand side what appeared to be a village of modern bungalows.

'What are those houses over there, Gladys?' I asked.

'Oh, those belong to the American forces,' she replied. 'The military authorities build those for servicemen's families. Nice aren't they?'

'Lovely,' I said. 'What a pity a whole lot more couldn't be built for all the people who are living in shacks.'

Even as I voiced this hope I realised how forlorn it was, for there were over three million refugees from the mainland of China living on the island, together with the eight million Taiwanese. The population of the island, measuring only 13,808 square miles, was at that time over eleven million.

As our taxi reached the village of Peitou, I noticed that the paddy fields were now terraced and the countryside looked green and beautiful in the morning sunshine. We drove on up the mountainside towards the Children's Home with azalea plants on each side of the road – not yet in flower. There seemed to be masses of luscious green shrubs, looking healthy and fertile because of the hot springs nearby. We could see the steam from them rising to great heights and I was to discover later what a boon these springs were.

Here we were at last! Over the huge doors of what had been a hotel was the simple statement 'Gladys Aylward Children's Home'. We walked into the entrance hall and were soon surrounded by hordes of children who had been eagerly looking out for us.

The Superintendent and his wife greeted us and then introduced us to two other friends from England who were to join us for our celebrations. It was good to be able to speak to someone in English again.

Christmas celebrations now began in earnest, although it was four days after the event. Small groups of children sang and took part in little plays, and with the help of an old harmonium, they sang, in Chinese, a chorus which I had sung many times at home in the chapel that I had attended as a child: 'Wide wide as the ocean, high as the heavens above, deep deep as the deepest sea, is my Saviour's love.' I joined in with them in English, realising how wonderful indeed was the love of God. It *did* span the oceans. It had sent Gladys to the aid of needy Chinese orphans many years before, and now I had been sent to help her out of love for Him.

What fun we had that day! The children loved dressing up and entered into the spirit of Christmas as only children can. Mary and Joseph looked most impressive as they tenderly cared for the doll which was Baby Jesus. The Shepherds bowed low in adoration before Him. They had all practised so hard because their 'mother' had returned from England specially to be with them. Their little eyes constantly sought hers for reassurance that they were doing well. Gladys revelled in it as she chatted with first one child, then another; as she took this baby into her arms, handed him to me or one of the other grown-ups, and took up another.

Time raced on and soon it was lunch time. We had the

usual bowls of rice with extra tit-bits as it was Christmas. Our English friends stayed on and, at tea time, offered to take us back to Taipei in their car. We arrived home feeling very tired but happy.

During the next week we visited the Home again because I was anxious to check up on the sponsoring of all the children and to see their case histories. I hoped also to have a chat with the Superintendent. He had already sent a batch of case histories to me shortly before I left Britain, but on browsing through them, I had noticed the numbering was very confused. In some cases duplicate numbers had been given to several of the children. I had brought the sheets to Taiwan with me to check up on them.

Gladys asked the Superintendent to bring the records down to her house the following Friday, so that I could go through them with him. We sat at Gladys's dining table and began checking the sheets which had been sent to me with the records he had brought. It was my intention to bring the records right up to date, taking a new photograph of each child to be pinned to its relative case history. The children could then be sponsored individually through our office in Britain.

But, as we began to check, a strange feeling came over me. There was something wrong. In the space of a few seconds, it seemed, first one child and then another 'disappeared'. 'Oh, that baby is no longer with us,' was one comment. 'Oh, that child left us the other day,' was another. In the next few minutes some twenty-five children disappeared, yet only three or four weeks earlier I had received their case history sheets in Britain when I had been asked to sponsor 120 children. It *now* seemed that there were only ninety-five real case histories and I smelled a rat!

When the Superintendent had returned to the Home, I said to Gladys, 'Do you think that man is honest?'

56

She turned abruptly and glared at me as she replied, 'Honest? Of course he's honest. He's my son-in-law.' I could read her mind – how dare I doubt his honesty!

I explained to her what had happened with the case histories and could see that she was as puzzled as I was. But she trusted this man and his wife. They had been running the Home for three or four years. They *must* be trustworthy.

Not wishing to upset her any more, I said, 'Well, I won't say anything else for the moment, Gladys, but I suggest that we keep our eyes open and ask God to show us if there *is* anything wrong.'

8
The lull before the storm

Before Gladys's last British visit, the Children's Home had been supported by an American organisation, World Vision, which had been very helpful. They had arranged tours for her in America, Canada, Australia and New Zealand and, as a result, a lot of money had come in to build a permanent home for her children. She had written to me, at one stage, from America saying that she had never been so well cared for in all her life – her American friends were absolutely wonderful to her.

Unfortunately, now that she was back in Taiwan, there seemed to be some misunderstanding with World Vision. The new Children's Home was being built, but it was doubtful whether it would be handed over to Gladys. The reason for this we simply could not understand. I had to get to the bottom of it all.

In the next week or two we discovered a great number of reasons why our American friends were concerned, and that our Chinese friends shared these worries also.

First of all Esther Huang, Gladys's close friend, came to visit us. It was early in the morning for a social visit and from her manner, it was clear she had come on a special mission. There was no time today for the lengthy Chinese formalities of enquiring how everyone was before getting down to the *real* reason for the visit.

Gladys immediately guessed Esther must have something important to say, so they disappeared into the privacy of her small bedroom. It was quite some time before they reappeared and Gladys was solemn as she bade her friend goodbye.

Deep in thought, she came into the small living-room and sat down. I waited, knowing that if she intended to tell me anything she would do so in her own good time.

After a few moments' reflection, she looked up. 'Do you know what Esther said?' She hesitated, appearing to be thinking aloud more than communicating with me. She went on, 'Esther said that while I was in Britain, God had told her to pray for Gladys Aylward, particularly on her return to Taiwan, for then Gladys Aylward would face one of the greatest trials of her life.'

Gladys waited for the impact of her words to sink in. I could see that she could hardly take in the message either.

I voiced tentatively the first question that sprang to my mind, 'Did she give any inkling of what it was about?'

'No,' Gladys replied. 'Esther does not know herself. She only knows that God is warning us.'

I felt sick, my mind full of foreboding.

What *was* going on? If only I knew the language, I could ask a few questions. As it was, I had to glean what I could from scraps of conversation repeated to me in English! How would I ever get to the bottom of this strange mystery, I asked myself.

Though we were both anxious to know what the 'trial' was to be – our enquiries progressed slowly and, as so often happens, there was a lull before the storm.

Gladys had already arranged for us to stay with her adopted elder son, Jarvis, in Chiayi. Perhaps he would be able to enlighten us. We would go down to Chiayi, as arranged, for Jarvis or someone else down there might know far more than we did.

From what we had deduced so far, doubts seemed to centre around the Children's Home and the persons running it. I thought again of the case histories of the children which I had tried to check. It was no use saying anything more about these at the moment. It would be better to go to Chiayi. In any case, away from home, it would be easier to see things in their true perspective and pray about the situation.

That Saturday evening, 18th January, Chi Kuang had been put to bed an hour earlier and Gladys had gone to check that he was still asleep, when as I sat alone in her living-room, I had the strangest sensation of movement. The pictures on the walls seemed to shake before my very eyes.

'What on earth is happening?' I said as Gladys came back from the bedroom.

'Sit tight,' she replied. 'It's only an earthquake.'

Only an earthquake! How *could* she be so calm? The more I got to know Gladys and her Chinese fellow-citizens, the more I was amazed at their resilience in the face of everyday problems of life which would appal us in the West. We don't know how fortunate we are.

Gladys decided that on the way to Chiayi, we could call in at Puli to see Barbara and, as Sun Moon Lake, the well known beauty spot, was in the vicinity of Puli too, it would give her an opportunity of showing off some of the beauties of her adopted homeland.

A day or two later we waved goodbye to Chi Kuang and Yang So and took a pedicab to the station. On arrival I was very amused to hear loudspeakers blaring forth 'Home, home on the range, where the deer and the antelope play.' Perhaps it was for the benefit of the American forces, but it certainly sounded strange on a Chinese railway station!

We boarded the train for Taichung and arrived there about three hours later. Then we boarded the Golden Horse Express bus to Puli. The journey took about two hours and the scenery was beautiful. At first the road took us between paddy fields and groves of sugar-cane. Then banana trees began to appear, the big bunches of

60

unripe green fruit hardly discernible against the huge leaves which hung down gracefully. The road wound upwards and the hillside paddy-fields became terraced. In the distance we could see the Changyang Shan Me, their lofty peaks standing out against the brilliant blue sky.

At last we reached Puli where Barbara met us and we saw the large mission hospital of which she was matron. I wondered how the American organisation, having found such an ideal spot, had managed to get all the building materials to this out-of-the-way place up the narrow road on which we had travelled.

After seeing Barbara, we spent two nights in Puli at the home of an elderly German couple who had been missionaries on the mainland of China for years. When the Communists took over and they had to leave, instead of retiring to a more comfortable life back home in Germany, they had decided that God wanted them in Taiwan. So here they were in this small village, communicating their faith in Jesus to the people.

The following day we had a magnificent trip to Sun Moon Lake. Apparently there were two lakes originally – the Sun and the Moon – but the Japanese, during their occupation of the island, had dammed the lakes' exits so that the water could be used to generate electric power. The waters rose and the lakes became one – Sun Moon Lake. It lay only a few miles from Puli and to get there we again took the Golden Horse bus. The road twisted and turned and as we gained height, became rougher, but the scenery more picturesque. Tree-covered hills were interspersed with low valleys. In no time at all we reached our destination.

I drank in the beauty of that idyllic spot. The waters of the lake appeared clear blue in the morning sunshine. A tiny island stood in the middle, on which sat a small shrine. High mountains and wooded hills stood out as a back-drop to the picture, making it seem unreal, as if someone had painted the whole scene on a canvas. It was incredibly beautiful. I was glad I had brought my camera to record all I saw and especially grateful to three little girls who posed for a picture in their traditional costumes.

Gladys suggested we go to the Evergreen hostel, overlooking the lake, for lunch. As we climbed up to it, I found it was not a hostel at all but a comfortable hotel.

We returned to Puli in time for tea at the mission hospital with Barbara and some of her colleagues and, the next day, left for Chiayi in the afternoon. By the time we had caught the Golden Horse bus back to Taichung and then got a train connection to Chiayi, it was later than we intended. To make matters worse, it began to rain heavily. At the station Gladys hailed a pedicab and asked the man to take us to Jarvis's home. Because of the weather the hood of the pedicab was pulled up and an oilskin sheet attached to it and draped down in front of us. We could hardly breathe as we sat cramped up with our cases at our feet and bags on our knees.

We swayed crazily in the dark as the pedicab man pedalled along furiously. Suddenly he stopped, lifted the sheet, and announced that he was lost. After a hasty consultation, Gladys 'sorted him out' and he decided to have one more try at locating Jarvis's home. Gladys and I sat in the back giggling like two schoolgirls at the thought of going around half the night in a pedicab in the pouring rain.

The pedicab stopped again. To our relief we had arrived at our destination. Jarvis and his wife, Haiphong, gave us a great welcome. Their home had been damaged by the earthquake and there was plaster off the walls and cracks all over the place, so they had arranged for us to stay with two missionary ladies nearby. As the hour was late, Jarvis took us to their home and they couldn't have been more kind.

We had a good night's rest and, as the weather was clear again, we went along to visit Jarvis and his family. He was serving in the Free Chinese Air Force but had managed to secure two days off as his 'mother' was visiting him. He was one of Gladys's original adopted children from China, and had come out through Hong Kong when the Communists took over the mainland. He and his wife were both committed Christians and a very fine couple indeed.

Gladys chatted away with them in Mandarin Chinese whilst I sat and waited. During her conversation, she tried to discover whether he knew anything of the mystery which surrounded the Children's Home in Peitou. It seemed that he, too, had heard rumours that all was not well but could not put his finger on what was wrong. If he heard any more and could throw any light on the situation, he promised that he would certainly let us know.

After lunch it was decided that we should go to visit two villages nearby which had been rather badly affected by the earthquake. The first one we came to was Pei Cur. It looked just as if it had suffered an air raid. I was staggered at the amount of damage. The villagers who had survived were living on the streets under crude coverings of zinc sheets and bamboo poles. A number of them were pottering about in the remains of what had once been their homes, trying in vain to locate something of value. It was a pathetic sight!

In the next village of Pei Ho we came across a large Buddhist temple which had been struck by the earthquake. I had got used to seeing colourful temples of all shapes and sizes on my travels, but in Pei Ho twelve nuns had been killed when one side of their temple had been ripped out and huge stone pillars fell to the ground, broken like matchsticks. The nuns and priests who survived, were working away with great zeal trying to rebuild the temple as fast as possible, hoping this would placate the gods. How I longed that they might be introduced to the living Lord Jesus Christ so that their superstitions might be replaced by a faith that would see them through all the exigencies of life.

After spending two nights in Chiayi and seeing as much as possible of Jarvis and his family, we journeyed back to Taipei on the eleven o'clock train, arriving there at about 3.30 p.m. Chi Kuang was overjoyed to see his 'Mummy' again and Yang So gave us a heart-warming welcome. It was good to be home, to open the mail and to settle down again to normal routine. We realised that now we must come down to earth, for we still had to discover the truth about the situation in the Children's Home.

9
The storm breaks

Shortly after our return from the south, another of Gladys's 'sons' visited us, and confirmed that he had also heard vague rumours about the Children's Home, though he did not know what it was all about. What had been going on? we wondered.

Then, as we sat talking, I looked around the room and caught sight of an object which had been bothering me ever since our arrival. Near Gladys's living-room door stood a safe which I had never seen her open once. It seemed a very public place to keep such an object, particularly if she wanted to leave money in it while she was away from home. Perhaps the safe was not hers ... perhaps it was the clue to the deepening mystery about the Home?

'Is it wise to keep a safe in your home when you are away so often?' I asked Gladys suddenly.

'Oh that is not mine,' she replied. 'Wong, the Superintendent, must have bought it while I was away. I don't know what for, but he lived here whilst I was in Britain and had some of the babies and a Chinese nurse from the Home living next door. I wonder why he did not take it away with him when he moved back into the house next door.'

Even as she spoke, our suspicions were aroused and we all jumped up and went to look at the safe. It was, of course, locked. What could be in it?

Gladys and Chiang decided to move the safe into my

bedroom and keep the bedroom door locked so that Wong and his wife would be unable to open the safe without Gladys's permission and supervision. During the next half hour we looked as if we were acting in some mystery film, as we hauled and dragged the heavy safe into my bedroom. When it was stowed away, we came out and Gladys locked the door and handed me the key.

'Now you keep the key, Vera,' she said, 'so that if I am asked where the safe is, I can honestly say that you have the key and I cannot get into your room.'

After our exhausting efforts we enjoyed a cup of China tea together before saying goodbye to Chiang, and thanking him for his help. I was not too sure that I liked the idea of sleeping in the same room as the safe. I only hoped that no one would try to retrieve it during the following night!

The next morning matters began to come to a head. As I sat in Gladys's living-room thinking of our antics of the night before, Wong appeared in the doorway. He gave me a nod and a smile as he passed through the living-room to look for Gladys. She was in the kitchen talking to Yang So.

I could hear voices and Gladys and Wong came back to the living-room. As he talked to Gladys, his gaze flitted from her face to mine. I could not understand a word of what they said, but I sensed that Wong appeared somewhat uneasy. He did not stay long as he was on his way to the Children's Home having spent the previous night with his wife and family in the house next door. Had he heard us humping around the safe the night before, I asked myself.

Later that day, Wong's wife also flitted in to see Gladys. She seemed anxious and on the lookout for something as she wandered through to the kitchen, ostensibly to retrieve a pan which she had lent to Yang So. But it was clear she was really looking for the whereabouts of that safe. No word of it was mentioned, however, as she made her way back home next door.

A few days later, while I was at the hairdresser's, Wong's wife came again and *asked* Gladys where the safe was. Gladys told her that she had moved it into my room.

'I would like to get something out of it,' the Chinese woman said.

'I can't get into the room. Vera has the key as it's her bedroom, and she is out,' replied Gladys in a matter-of-fact way. What else could Mrs. Wong do but return to her own home? Her common sense must have told her that Gladys's suspicions had been aroused.

Then a new turn of events helped to enlighten us even more. For a few days after our return from the south, I had not been at all well, so Gladys suggested that I should visit a missionary doctor for a check-up. He made various tests and asked me to go back to see him again in about a week, but while at the doctor's house, we got into conversation about the Home.

'How are you getting on with your work over here?' he asked.

'To be quite honest, I'm not sure,' I replied. 'I have a feeling that Gladys and I are heading for trouble with the man who is in charge of the Home.

To my astonishment, the doctor said, 'I am not at all surprised.'

'What *do* you mean?' I exclaimed.

'Well, when Gladys was in Britain, the people who were overseeing the work were not too happy either. They felt that man was not trustworthy,' he replied.

We chatted for a while and then I left his surgery to take a pedicab home. The pedicab man I hailed, nodded his agreement when I showed him the address to which I wished to go, and the number of Taiwanese dollars I intended to give him for the journey. Skilfully he manoeuvred his way at speed through the traffic. Deep in thought, my mind was going over all that the doctor had told me until suddenly, we came to a full stop and I almost fell out. We were face to face with a small red taxi and the drivers of both vehicles glared at each other and then started to shout. Neither would give way! To crown everything, the pedicab man got off his bicycle which drew my pedicab along and went to shelter from the hot sun under a shack nearby which served as a shop.

I sat in all my glory in the pedicab not knowing what to do. By now a small crowd had gathered, anxious to find out what was wrong. An elderly man, summing up the situation in a minute, obliged by moving the pedicab in which I still sat, to let the taxi pass. But still the pedicab man would not return.

Anxious to relate to Gladys, as soon as possible, my conversation with the doctor, I got out and started to walk in the direction of home. At this the crowd roared with laughter and cheered. The pedicab man, realising that he was about to lose his fare, pedalled after me as hard as he could. I pretended at first that I had not seen him and continued to walk on. After all, he must learn not to ditch his passengers when only half the journey was done. Then I turned and smiled. He smiled in return, stopped his cab and I stepped in. The remainder of the journey was uneventful.

Making my way into Gladys's home, I told her of my conversation with the missionary doctor. We were still not sure what action to take or just how the problem could be tackled. Two or three days later, however, God spoke to Gladys very clearly.

She was preparing for bed and had picked up her copy of *Daily Light*, to read a few verses. The verse at the top of the page jumped out at her. She called to me: 'Vera, can you come here a minute?'

I wondered what she could be so anxious about at this time of night, so I went into her bedroom at once.

'Read that,' she said. 'We've got to do something.'

She thrust the *Daily Light* into my hands and I read: 'But if ye will not drive out the inhabitants of the land from before you; then it shall come to pass, that those which ye let remain of them shall be pricks in your eyes and thorns in your sides, and shall vex you in the land wherein ye dwell' (Numbers 33 v. 55).

Yes, it was quite obvious what God had said. We *had* to do something.

We discussed the matter again and decided that the very next day we would have to tackle Wong and his wife, first enlisting the moral support of the missionary doctor. We prayed together and asked God for wisdom in this very difficult situation. We knew we had to act, but how and where did we begin? We went to bed in the confidence that our Heavenly Father would show us.

Next morning, I was conscious of the feeling that we had an unpleasant day ahead of us. Immediately we had breakfasted, I went to get the assistance of the missionary doctor. Explaining to him what had happened the night before, I asked whether he could come over to Gladys's home and give us his support. He gladly agreed to do what he could to help, and promised to join us after lunch that day.

Meantime, Gladys, knowing that Wong would be coming down from Peitou to spend the weekend with his wife and children, went to the house next door to ask Mrs. Wong to join us with her husband after lunch.

As we ate our lunch we were thoughtful, wondering what was the best way to challenge Wong and his wife. It was fairly obvious the money sent by Gladys to be used for new equipment for the Home had not been invested in this way. With Gladys's help I had totalled up the number of cheques and amount of money sent to him. Until now, Gladys had not realised just how much she *had* sent. In the past, she had trusted him so implicitly that it had never occurred to her to question what he had done with the money.

She had no head for business and out of the generosity of her heart she had passed on to him many of her own personal gifts as well as gifts earmarked for the Home. What could he have done with the large amounts of money sent to him? This was the question now uppermost in our minds.

As we finished lunch, we were relieved to see the missionary doctor reach Gladys's house first. We went into my bedroom as we felt the first thing to do was to ask Wong to open the safe.

A few minutes later, Wong and his wife arrived. Gladys went out to meet them and brought them into the bedroom too. As we all assembled, Wong seemed to realise his worst fears had come true. It was written all over his face. Gladys Aylward, his wife's adopted mother, would never have suspected anything by herself. This English woman, with her ability to understand figures, was up to something, he was sure.

Gladys turned to Wong and his wife and spoke to them in Chinese, the doctor very quietly interpreting for me. Mrs. Wong went over to the safe, pretended to be unlocking it, then announced that it would not open! The doctor promptly offered to help her. He took the keys and in a matter of seconds the safe stood open and the contents were taken out. There was very little money but there were deeds of a house purchase! What had they done with all the money Gladys had sent to them? Gladys pleaded with the Chinese couple to tell her. The doctor pleaded with them, but the couple maintained a stony, defiant silence.

More conversation took place in Chinese between Gladys and the doctor and again she pleaded with the couple. But it seemed that nothing would budge them. They refused to say a word.

70

Still Gladys pleaded. At last, Wong said that he did not have any money because he had spent it all on the Home: the small box taken from the safe with the deeds contained only his own personal papers. He seemed obdurate.

One thought had occurred to me, however. I said, turning to Gladys, 'Could we not call the police?'

At the mention of the word 'police' Wong found his tongue.

'Yes, I have got the money,' he confessed. 'It is in the Post Office.'

At this his wife began to weep and to wail, kneeling at Gladys's feet and pleading with her not to bring the law into the matter.

The doctor was far more practical. 'Where are the Post Office books showing the amount deposited?' he asked.

Wong pointed to the small box which had been taken out of the safe. He took a small key from his pocket, opened the box and handed over the two books. The doctor and Gladys scrutinised them, soon realising that there were several hundred pounds in two accounts in Wong's own name!

Gladys turned on the couple with a tirade of Chinese, her Cockney sense of justice outraged. It went against the grain for her, but people in Britain had given sacrificially for the orphans, and it was up to her to see that this money was used for that purpose. Why should it go into the pocket of an avaricious man with no conscience?

The Chinese couple, surprised at Gladys's wrath, stood in guilty silence. They could not have known that Gladys's 'Girl Friday' had had a business training and knew how to check accounts. But they realised that dear simple Gladys was no longer alone, and could not be hoodwinked any longer.

Finally, exasperated, Gladys ordered them out of the house. They disappeared as fast as they could, not bothering to ask for the safe, the keys or the Post Office books.

The doctor offered to take us to the chief Post Office in Taipei immediately to endeavour to recover the money. On reaching the building with him, we were taken through a maze of rooms to the office of the man in charge. The whole story was explained to him by the doctor and Gladys. He agreed to refund the money from one account immediately and handed over £500. The money in the other account could not be drawn out, because it had been placed on special deposit for a month. The chief cashier assured us, however, that he would 'freeze' it so that it could not be drawn out by Wong meantime. The doctor promised to keep the money already withdrawn in his own safe until suitable arrangements could be made for it to be used or invested in the Home.

When the doctor dropped us off at Gladys's gate we felt completely and utterly exhausted! But there was no time to relax, for Gladys decided that we must go up to the Children's Home, at once, to look in the safe there. She was like a bloodhound hot on the scent, wanting to find whether there was any more money tucked away. Into the house next door she went, and reappeared in a matter of seconds with Wong. Then she hailed a passing taxi and we motored up to Peitou in painful silence.

Once inside the Home, Gladys headed for the office-cum-bedroom which had been occupied by Wong. Yes, there was that 'other' safe. She asked Wong to open it and he obeyed with very bad grace. There was a little money inside which Wong insisted was his own. They were only a few Taiwanese dollars and not worth arguing about, so Gladys allowed him to pocket them. But that was not all – she insisted that the staff be informed that the Superintendent had been dismissed. The surprise on their faces was evident.

Before Wong disappeared to make his own way home, only too anxious to escape from those accusing, penetrating dark eyes, Gladys made it clear that she expected him to return on Monday morning to clean out all the papers in the drawers and to explain about the sponsoring of the children. At last, we wearily made our way back to Taipei to take our evening meal with Chi Kuang and Yang So.

It had been a shattering experience, for Gladys especially. We sat together in her little home that evening feeling worn out by the day's events. The thought of what might happen on the morrow had not yet occurred to us.

After a few minutes' reflection, Gladys turned to me and said: 'Do you realise one of us has got to take over the Children's Home tomorrow?'

I hadn't, but as my mind grappled with the thought, I realised that she was due to speak at a retreat in the mountains the following day.

I replied, 'Well, as you have speaking engagements all day tomorrow, it looks as if it's going to be me, doesn't it?'

'I'm afraid so,' she said.

I was aghast. How could *I* possibly run the Home? I didn't even speak Chinese! But, as far as Gladys was concerned, that was all there was to it. So she turned her attention to the post which had arrived earlier and which we had not had time to open.

As there was no mail for me, I lapsed into anxious thought. How *would* I cope? How would we both cope?

Suddenly Gladys exclaimed, 'Oh, how wonderful!' She was reading an air letter from England and when she had finished she handed it over to me.

It was more than wonderful; it was nothing short of miraculous! Here was a letter from Nottingham, from a lady named Kathleen Langton Smith, asking whether she could help in the Children's Home. Kathleen had met

Gladys at the Albert Hall, Nottingham, during our trip together and since that time had felt sure God wanted her to work in Taiwan.

On the very day that we had had to dismiss the Superintendent, our Heavenly Father had provided another of His servants for the task. We went to bed with hearts full of thanksgiving, in spite of the awful ordeal we had been through.

10
96 children overnight!

The next morning, which was a Sunday, I packed my new green case in some trepidation, for I must be ready to go to the Children's Home while Gladys was going to the retreat.

Suddenly there was a commotion at the door. Two men were standing there with a new bed, which we had forgotten we had ordered some weeks before. The one on which I was sleeping had collapsed a number of times, much to my consternation!

Did they *have* to deliver it on a Sunday? I thought, and particularly on this Sunday! We had no option but graciously to accept the delivery.

Soon someone else was at the door.

Could we take a new baby into the Children's Home, a man asked. Gladys had a hurried consultation with him and away he went.

At last we were free. Gladys and I said goodbye to each other.

'I hope you have a wonderful time at the retreat, Gladys,' I said.

'Thank you, dear,' she replied. 'I know you will be all right up at the Home. The Lord will be with you. I will try to come up and see you tomorrow.'

I was in a daze as I got into the taxi. How was I – a 'Girl Friday' – going to cope? We went on the now familiar route up to Peitou and in about half an hour I arrived at the old hotel – The Gladys Aylward Children's Home.

As I walked through the front door, I breathed a silent prayer, 'Help me, dear Lord, I haven't a clue where to begin!'

Then I began by using my common sense.

I went to see the children – starting in the nursery with the youngest. There were five tiny babies in their beds and three toddlers in a play-pen. Two Chinese *amahs* (nurses) were caring for them. I cooed and played with the babies for a short while and the *amahs*, sensing my love for children, put one after another into my arms. I wanted to gain the confidence of the children and nurses. The latter were not professionally trained, but women from the nearby village who, having had children of their own, knew exactly what to do for these homeless mites.

I looked around. The nursery was bare and very smelly. It would be a good idea to clean the place up. First of all, why not bath the babies? There seemed to be only two towels in the room, so I went across the yard to the storeroom for more. Gladys had given me the key so that I could help myself to whatever I thought was needed. I rummaged around until I found a supply of colourful towels and some nice new nappies, all of which had obviously been sent by friends in America.

On my return to the nursery, the faces of the women lit up at the welcome sight of new things. I smiled and showed by my actions that I wanted each baby and toddler to have its own towel. They nodded and smiled in return. Next I went to the Japanese hot spring bath, just across the corridor, and brought in some warm water. I gently took up each baby and toddler in turn and bathed them and put nappies on them all. None of the toddlers had been wearing nappies and the result can be imagined! The babies cried at first, for they were used to seeing a tanned face leaning over them. Whoever can this white-faced person be, they must have thought.

The *amahs* then went to fetch clean clothes for the children. Before they dressed them, I indicated I would prefer them all to wear nappies until they were toilet trained.

Next, one of the *amahs* fetched the cleaning man who came with his mop and bucket. I could even provide some disinfectant for the floors, because Gladys had made sure that I took up an ample supply that very morning, together with baby cream and other necessities. Soon the nursery was clean and spotless and so were the babies.

As the days went by, Gladys and I discovered that quite a show had been put on at the Home when we were expected; but on other days, things had been allowed to slide.

Sadly, it had never occurred to Gladys to doubt the ability of the Chinese couple who had been running the Home. The fact that it was not well equipped with the latest gadgets, was not for lack of energy on her part. She spent her whole life taking meetings, all over the world, and doing all she could to provide money for necessities. It never entered her head that she should keep a strict note of what money she had sent on to Wong. The Home should have been an orphanage *par excellence*, had every penny Gladys provided gone into the running of it.

As I looked with satisfaction around the clean nursery, I realised that we had visitors. One of the Chinese girls who helped to care for the older age group, came through with some American people who had heard of the famous ex-parlourmaid and her children's home. It was good to be able to talk again to someone in my own tongue. I explained that I had taken over only that morning, and showed them around, realising more and more what a colossal task was ahead of us. So much equipment was needed. Where did we begin?

When the visitors had gone I went into the office which was now to be my room. It must be tidied out before I made my bed. It was the normal Taiwanese kind of bed – a wooden frame with a hard rattan base. Not the most comfortable to sleep on, they take a little getting used to. However, after the one which I had in Taipei, this one looked comparatively safe.

There was a knock at the door and a smiling Chinese girl stood there with my lunch – a bowl of steaming hot rice with meat and vegetables on top. I smiled my thanks and sat down to enjoy my solitary meal, though I was still finding it difficult to adjust to rice two or three times a day.

After lunch, quietness descended upon the Home while everyone took their afternoon nap. It was too hot to do anything but sleep so I decided to follow suit. I was glad of the peace and solitude and felt refreshed.

When things began to stir later in the afternoon, being at a loss to know what to do next, I started to clean out the large cupboard in my room. It contained quite a store of small baby clothes, many of them hand-made, possibly by friends in other lands. To my dismay, most of them had tiny holes in them. Was it moths? I discovered later that mice had done the damage!

In the cupboard I also found an old copy of *Keswick Week* talks. What a Godsend! Here was something that I could read in the evenings when things had quietened down again. I had often visited Keswick when I worked in the Lake District. Every year a Convention is held there in July – and these were some of the talks in print.

Darkness fell suddenly at about 6 p.m. I missed the twilight that we were so used to at home, but I was now getting accustomed to the sudden change. Earlier, I had noticed tiny green lizards darting about the ceiling of the

78

room. Now that it was dark, they came out in force. Gladys had told me they were harmless and it was better to leave them alone, as they fed on the mosquitoes which were so prevalent in this hot climate. I was not too happy, though, when they played their games right over my bed. It would not be pleasant to find them *in* the bed during the night!

I was soon engrossed in my *Keswick Week*. As I became more hot and sticky in the humid, sultry evening atmosphere, I imagined that I was once again in that cool and lovely place, walking along by Derwentwater, regarded by many as the most beautiful lake in the whole of the Lake District.

As I read on, I felt inspired and encouraged. I knew in my heart that Christ, who had led me here, would give me the strength and wisdom to tackle this new chapter in my life. So, I went to bed with a peaceful heart – only to be awakened in the middle of the night by strange noises. Better get up and investigate, I decided.

I slipped on my coat, unlocked my door and went along the corridor into the courtyard. Everything was very still and quiet, except for the crickets singing their nightly chorus. I would never have believed that they were so loud! All seemed to be well, so I went back to bed and after a while settled off to sleep again.

My slumbers were disturbed again before long, by the crying of babies. The nursery was next door to my room and the sound carried easily through the wall. As I knew a Chinese *amah* was on night duty, I felt it would be unwise to interfere and slept fitfully after that until dawn.

I greeted the day joyfully, in spite of my broken night, because I knew that Gladys was coming up to the Home with Chi Kuang. It would be good to see them.

They arrived at 9 a.m. and soon afterwards Wong reappeared. He was anxious to collect his personal belongings from the room in which we were working. One look at his expression told us that he was in a very bad humour. He had been found out and lost face, which was something no Chinese person could ever accept. Gladys greeted him coldly.

Wong began to clean out the drawers, tearing up papers and scattering them about the floor of the room, hoping that this tantrum would indicate to us more than words how infuriated he felt.

He refused also to hand over any case histories of the children, to provide us with accounts as to how much money he had received from Gladys or how it had been spent. He could not have been more unco-operative. When he had gathered together his belongings, he swept out of the room, picking his way through the debris which he had thrown across the floor with a triumphant grin as if to say, 'Clear *that* up and see what you can find.'

After his departure, we spent the rest of the morning trying to discover how best we could run the place until Kathleen's arrival. Gladys talked first with the staff – the three Chinese *amahs*, the three 'teachers' who cared for the older children, the cook, the man who assisted him, the cleaning man, the sewing woman and the washer-woman – eleven in all. They were all doing a good job, especially the washer-woman, washing by hand day after day for ninety-six children. She must be a gem! I thought.

All seemed in order with the staff, and one of the teachers explained that she had case histories for all the children, except one – a baby girl.

'And where are her papers?' asked Gladys.

'The Superintendent has them,' replied the girl. 'The new baby only came into the home last month.'

Gladys enquired from the rest of the staff, but no one seemed to know where the child had come from, how old she was or what her name was. She was a beautiful little girl but unhappy because she was obviously suffering

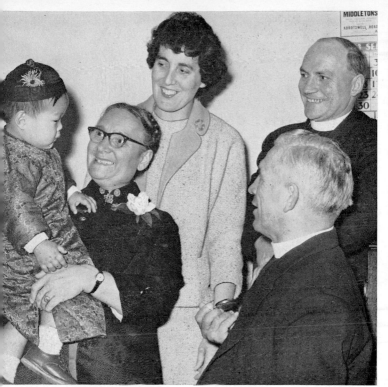

enjoyed travelling round Britain with Gladys and Gordon
(Copyright *Aberdeen Journals Ltd*)

Gladys was surprised that anyone should want to watch her on television

(*BBC copyright photograph*)

Gordon obliged photographer by eating up his banana and smiling broadly

(*copyright Belfast News-Letter Ltd*)

Pedicabs were a favourite form of transport in Taiwan

Gladys and I enjoyed our Christmas in Kowloon

The children of Hong Kong were adorable

vernight I found myself in charge of ninety-six Chinese
hildren

ordon and my adopted daughter Jade were like brother
ad sister

Kathleen Langton Smith (centre) continues to run the smaller
children's home in Taipei

Jade soon settled down in
our flat in England
(*copyright Syndicate International*)

As my bridesmaid, she
looked as pretty as a pictu
(*copyright Evening Sentinel,
Stoke-on-Trent*)

from malnutrition. She had a prickly heat rash on her face and what appeared to be small boils on her head. Gladys guessed that she would be about fourteen months old and, as she had to have a name, I decided to call her Ruth meantime.

Some of the other babies were not too well either; a number had the same prickly heat rash. I felt that they had far too many clothes on at night in the hot climate but, as far as the *amahs* were concerned, it was winter and in their view the children must be well wrapped up. 'If this is winter, what on earth is it like in summer?' I thought.

After tea, Gladys and Chi Kuang left to go home to Taipei, but she promised to come up again at the weekend. During the rest of that week I did what I could, though, not being able to communicate with anyone, this was far from easy. I spent some time in the store sorting out clothes, and the young 'teachers' were most helpful, bringing to me any child they felt desperately needed something new. I also tackled the prickly heat rash with some medicine one of them obtained from a shop in the village, and my TCP ointment came to my aid to tackle the boils on little Ruth's head.

She was an insecure child, and responded so much to my efforts to help her that every time I went into the nursery, she would put out her thin little arms indicating that she wanted me to pick her up. The other babies were sweet too. I became very fond of them all as, with my sparse medical knowledge, I sought to help and heal them.

I realised again and again how much more important deeds were than words. I was getting to know my new family even though I couldn't speak their language. They felt that I cared and I was conscious of this.

At the end of my first week as 'acting superintendent', I was due to visit the missionary doctor again. I travelled down to Taipei on the bus with a light heart and took a pedicab out to the doctor's surgery. As was the custom, on arrival, I took off my shoes and changed into a pair of mules, various sizes of which were laid out on the doorstep. Our doctor greeted me as I entered his surgery, and I sat down completely relaxed and totally unprepared for his next words.

'I'm afraid you have symptoms of cancer,' he said. 'I would like you to enter a mission hospital here in Taipei for an examination under anaesthetic. If it is malignant, you will have to go home on the next plane, if it isn't, we can think again!'

Was I hearing aright? My heart began to pound and my legs felt like jelly. This couldn't be happening to *me*! The conversation continued and I felt dazed. 'On what date can you enter the hospital?' enquired the doctor.

I got out my diary and we decided that the best time would be two and a half weeks later. The doctor, knowing that this news had been a shock, suggested that I stay to lunch with him and his wife. I gladly accepted.

His wife was delightful, and over lunch I gained some crumbs of comfort from my conversation with her. After all, with modern medical knowledge, cancer could often be cured if found in time, and people had been known to live for years afterwards ...

After lunch I thanked them for being so helpful and kind and travelled back to the Children's Home in a mental daze. It took me ages to walk up the mountainside from the bus to the 'old hotel'. My legs felt like lead.

My mind was in a turmoil as I went into my room and question after question flooded my brain. How could God let a thing like this happen to me when we had so much trouble on our hands anyway? How was Gladys going to be able to cope if I had to go home?

My heart raced as I tried to grapple with the enormity of this turn of events. I couldn't think clearly and it seemed as if the very devil himself was tempting me to abandon my faith. 'Aren't you a fool?' he seemed to say. 'Fancy leaving a good job at the university to come out here to serve God, and then He lets you down like this. There is no God, or He would never have let this happen. You might just as well give up your faith here and now. This is the end. You haven't long to live anyway, if you have got cancer.'

I don't know how long I sat there trying to think things out. There was no-one I could talk to. I would not be seeing Gladys until the following day. Jesus was the only one with whom I *could* have a conversation. I dropped on my knees and poured out my heart before Him. I told Him that I couldn't understand why He had allowed this to happen, especially when we had so much trouble on our hands already. It didn't seem fair, I explained, when I was doing my best to serve Him.

As I continued to pray, the thought came to me: 'Why *shouldn't* it happen to you? Why should *you* of all people be immune from the things other people suffer?' Why indeed? I had no more merit than anyone else in the whole wide world; less in fact.

I thought of the story in the Old Testament of how Naaman had been healed. I knew in my heart that God could heal me too, if it was His will.

Again I prayed: 'Lord Jesus I believe that you can heal me if it is your will and, as an act of faith, I am going into the Japanese bath across the corridor and dipping seven times, just as Naaman dipped seven times in the Jordan.'

Without more ado, and in all sincerity and earnestness, I did just that, proving to God that I still believed in Him and His power to heal. As I came out of the water the seventh time, I knelt on the steps of the bath and thanked God that He had already healed me. Knowing, however, that one cannot dictate to God, I added a rider and told

Him that if it was not His will to heal me, then I would serve Him for as long as He allowed me to live.

A wonderful peace flooded my heart and mind and I knew that the issue was with the Lord Jesus and that I must leave it there. My life was literally in His hands.

Knowing that Gladys was coming up to the Home the next day, I reflected on the past week. It had been difficult chiefly because I had not been able to talk to the Chinese staff. We had understood each other quite well with sign language, though, and we had had many good laughs together. I smiled and nodded and bowed to show them how much I appreciated their efforts. I would growl and shake my head from side to side to signify my disapproval. They never failed to get the message and our 'conversations' became quite a game. It had been nevertheless very exhausting.

When Gladys arrived the following day with Chi Kuang, I first related to her all that had happened at the doctor's.

'Oh, I don't suppose you have got it, dear,' she said. 'I'm sure it will be all right.'

She was so matter of fact and full of faith, I felt uplifted. Yes, God *was* in control. 'Don't think about it any more,' I told myself. Then I explained to her that I could not really run the Home indefinitely alone.

'Can we not get someone to come and help as interpreter and secretary?' I asked. 'It would make a world of difference.'

'Yes, that's a good idea,' she replied. 'I know the very one. I'm sure Kitty Lin, the girl you went to the hairdresser's with, would come and help you. She speaks quite good English. I will ask her when I go home tonight, and will come up here again tomorrow to let you know and to help a bit.'

It certainly seemed a solution. I knew that I must set up a double entry book-keeping system immediately, to try to find out just exactly how much it *did* take to run the Home. It was impossible to do this unless I had someone to interpret for me. At least my business training would come in useful if I could get the office organised. I had wondered why God hadn't sent out a nurse or a doctor to help Gladys, but now I realised she needed someone to help on the business side of things even more. It was not possible to run an establishment of this size unless it was well organised.

The following day Gladys reappeared with the good news that Kitty would be delighted to help during the week and would go home from Friday to Sunday nights.

Kitty was a charming Christian girl and we got on extremely well together. I would give her a sum of money each day and she, in turn, would hand this to the cook to buy the daily vegetables and other food supplies. I asked him, through Kitty, to bring a chit for everything he bought and Kitty would then translate this Chinese chit into English. In this way, I was able to keep track of all outgoing money, while noting any incoming gifts from local American friends on the island and the monthly amounts sent out to us from the Gladys Aylward Trust in Britain.

I was on familiar ground as I started my cash book and ledgers, for I had taken care of the financial side of things at the large youth centre for twelve years.

Kitty also helped me to check again the case histories of the children. It was essential. For example, we couldn't get 'Ruth', the baby without a name, sponsored by friends in Britain, unless we knew who she was, how old she was and where she came from. I was getting to know Ruth very well and she was getting to know me. She didn't cry so much now, which was a blessing. If one baby began to cry in the night, then the other seven in the nursery were inevitably awakened and it took some time to calm them down again.

Kitty and I decided that we must try to trace where Ruth came from as soon as possible. She went down to Taipei to ask the former Superintendent who had handed this particular baby into the Home. She returned with a name and address and we decided that on the next day we would set out on our search. We seemed to be getting somewhere, at last.

11
'She your baby.'

Fortunately it was ideal weather for our proposed journey. Kitty and I walked down the mountainside to the village of Peitou. The address which Kitty had been given was quite a long way out into the country. There were no buses or trains, so the only way to reach it was by pedicab.

We enjoyed the morning sunshine and the beauty of the countryside, except that every time we went through a village and passed a river or pond, the smell was intolerable. Adequate sewerage was obviously one of the main problems of the island! And yet this did not seem to deter the many foreign visitors who came to see its unsurpassed beauty.

We travelled for about an hour and a half before we reached our destination, another small village. Here Kitty made enquiries among the local people. The address we had been given was a barber's shop, we discovered, and we walked to it, surrounded by curious villagers.

As we entered the shop, it seemed as if the whole village followed us inside. They listened while Kitty had a brief chat with the man who owned the shop and found there was a family living behind the premises. He took us through and we met a man in the uniform of the Free Chinese Air Force. While children played at our feet as best they could in the cramped room, Kitty had a long conversation with him.

The man explained that he had thought of putting his

87

youngest child, aged two, in the Home as his wife had left him, but when he had approached the Superintendent some weeks before, he had decided not to take the matter any further. No, he was sorry, he could not help us. He had never heard of the child that Kitty described to him.

Our hearts sank. We had come all this way for nothing, it seemed. There was little else left for us to do but to wend our weary way home again in the pedicab. The sun was now beating down fiercely and the return journey was even more tiring.

But after a meal we felt refreshed and even more determined to discover where Ruth came from. We would have to wait a day or two, however, as Kitty was going home for Chinese New Year, the following day.

Chinese families usually gather on New Year's Eve for a family feast and everyone wants to be at home for it. This raised difficulties at the Home, for quite a number of staff wanted to be away, and Gladys had to sort out the problem, so that there was someone on hand to look after the children. She left it to the staff themselves to decide who should stay and who should go home.

Gladys came again to see how we were faring and when she arrived, she had great news. She had received a cable from Kathleen Langton Smith saying that she was willing to come out and take over the Home. She had certainly been quick off the mark. We were so grateful to know that God had provided someone just at the time when we needed her.

The next day I went down to visit Gladys in her home. There was an air of festivity as I travelled on the bus from Peitou to Taipei. Everyone had given their home an extra clean in readiness for the New Year celebrations and they were now on the streets, dressed in their best clothes. It was holiday time!

Firecrackers were going off in all directions making the most unnerving noise, when I got off the bus in Taipei.

Weird processions wended their way through busy streets with colourful models of lions and dragons, mostly made from paper flowers, swaying and dancing through the excited crowds. As the lions and dragons were carried aloft, the people danced alongside them. A clamorous band tried to make itself heard as well above the din; the Chinese certainly did nothing without noise and colour.

I escaped as soon as I could from the crowds and managed to get a pedicab to Gladys's home which was a haven of rest on such an exciting day, despite the fact that people dropped in to see her from time to time. For lunch we went to an American restaurant as this made a change from our usual Chinese diet.

Over lunch I told Gladys about the strange noises I heard from time to time in my bedroom at night up at Peitou.

'Do you think there are mice in my room Gladys?' I asked.

'Mice?' she replied. 'Oh, no it won't be mice, it will be rats.'

'*Rats!*' I said, horrified. 'How *could* they get in? However can I get rid of them?'

'They probably get in under the door,' she continued in a matter-of-fact voice. 'I'll get some traps so that you can catch them.'

She promised to bring them to the Home the following day, assuring me that the rats wouldn't do *me* any harm – they were only looking for food. Some consolation!

Gladys came up as promised armed with two rat traps! These were duly set in my room, tucked away in the corner so that tiny hands could not interfere with them.

I promised to go down to her the next morning, taking Ruth with me. She had not been at all well and we felt that she should see the missionary doctor. We agreed to meet at Gladys's home and go along to the surgery together.

The next morning as I awoke I was conscious of a noise in the corner of the room. I jumped out of bed and investigated. Yes, sure enough, there was a huge rat in the trap! I hurriedly dressed and dashed along the corridor to get the cleaning man so that he could remove it. He came in with a beaming face because he had set the trap the night before and obviously he'd done a good job. He took the trap away and removed the rodent, to my great relief.

I then went into the nursery to collect Ruth. She put out eager arms as I picked her up, and dressed her in a pretty hand-made green woollen dress which I had discovered in the store. She looked beautiful and was obviously happy to be with me. We travelled down to the town where we met Gladys and Chi Kuang. The doctor couldn't have been more helpful, and we left armed with the appropriate medicine and advice as to the course of action I should take.

As soon as we arrived at Gladys's home, we left Ruth with Chi Kuang and Yang So, and Gladys and I set out on a very important piece of investigation.

I had taken a second look at a visiting card Wong had given me on my arrival in Taiwan, which showed he had an office in Taipei. This was news to Gladys, and she was determined to find it. There was just one snag – the card gave only a telephone number. When I had expressed my doubts about the possibility of ever finding the office, Gladys had an idea.

'Before I left Taiwan for Britain,' she said, 'Wong had a friend whom I did not care for very much. A clock disappeared from my mission hall about a year ago and a few weeks later this friend, Ling, presented me with a clock exactly the same. After that I never felt I could trust him ... there was something about him that I did not like.'

So here we were, looking for Ling's home – because

we felt he must be in some way connected with Wong. When Gladys suddenly dived down a dark narrow close, I followed hard on her heels, not wishing to lose her in this somewhat dubious quarter of the town. Soon she entered a doorway and made her way, with great determination, up some steps to the front door of a flat.

She rapped on the door, head on one side and eyes alert like some eager blackbird, listening for the slightest noise.

Very quietly the door opened slightly and an elderly lady, dressed in black, peered out with beady eyes. She was obviously not taking any chances until she knew who it was. Gladys spoke to her through the crack in the door, her voice soothing as she tried to reassure her. Could we come in for a few minutes to talk to her, she eventually asked. After some persuasion the door opened and we entered.

Gladys took in the whole room at a glance. There was a partition down the middle; at the opposite end stood a table with a telephone on it. Gladys began to question the old lady who seemed to be vociferously denying any knowledge of Ling, for she shook her head from side to side as if anxious not to get involved in something she knew nothing about.

It was my chance. Realising the old woman's attention had been diverted by Gladys, I quietly made my way across the room to the telephone. Yes, the number was the one on Wong's card. At least we had discovered that much. I also surreptitiously peeped over the high partition. All I could see were large cardboard boxes stacked one on top of the other. It appeared that Wong and Ling were in some kind of business together.

Eventually, not wishing to upset the old woman unduly, for she might well be an innocent party to whatever was going on, Gladys thanked her warmly for allowing us to come in and she bowed us out with a beaming smile.

As we made our way back, I told Gladys of my discoveries, and she confirmed that the old lady had denied any knowledge of Ling. For the moment there did not seem to be anything we could do.

Back home, Yang So had prepared lunch for all of us and we spent the rest of the day together. Gordon loved having Ruth as a playmate. As she was not yet walking, he willingly brought small toys to her or took them away! It was very good for both of them: for Gordon – not to be the only one in the family; and for Ruth – to enjoy life in an ordinary home instead of a large establishment.

It was so late by the time that Ruth and I arrived back at the Home that all the children were already settled for the night. I decided that, in order not to disturb them, I would put Ruth in the cot in my room. She, of course, was delighted and lay there, cooing and laughing at all this personal attention.

But as the evening wore on, the prickly heat rash became more and more troublesome to her and she cried a good deal. I applied the medicine prescribed by the doctor and it soothed the inflamed spots on her face. But the boils on her head seemed to be getting worse though I consoled myself with the knowledge that all the infection would have to come away before her skin could heal. Finally at one o'clock she managed to go to sleep, as I patted her gently and quietly repeated 'Shui chiao, shui chiao – go to sleep.' In the morning she went back to the nursery quite happily.

Friends of the Home in the American forces stationed on the island had heard of our plight, and offers of help were coming in. It was heart-warming to welcome the servicemen's wives especially. We set them to work helping us clear out the huge clothes store nearby. It now had to serve as a sewing-room too, because we had had to take over the proper sewing-room for Kitty to sleep in. Some of the servicemen also came up, and began to decorate the place.

Our problems were certainly not over. We were having difficulties with the cook. A man appeared asking for money for rice and declaring that two previous lots of rice had not been paid for. When Gladys and Kitty got to the bottom of the story, we discovered that the cook had been stealing the rice for himself. We therefore gave him a month's pay, in lieu of notice, so that we could get rid of him as soon as possible.

As if that was not enough, there was more trouble to come! Baby clothes were disappearing faster than we could replace them. More enquiries revealed that one of the *amahs* had been taking them, so we had to ask her to go too. Through Kitty, she told me such a tale of woe about her husband in prison and four children in another orphanage, that I gave her two months' money in lieu of notice.

We had the good fortune to find another *amah* straight away – and she could speak a little English, which was a distinct advantage, for me at least. Meanwhile the rest of our Chinese staff were excellent and most reliable, and we greatly appreciated all their selfless service.

While Kitty was at home for Chinese New Year, she had managed to visit the previous Superintendent to ask about Ruth again. She not only returned with another address which we might contact, but she also discovered that the child's real name was Yu Ching. At least this was a beginning.

Gladys explained that Yu Ching meant in English 'Precious Jade' and I thought it a delightful name. We could at last call our baby by her proper name.

One of the American servicemen's wives offered to take us to the address Kitty had found, and the following week we set out in her huge salmon pink car to try to trace where Jade came from. We had to find Keelung, a town on the coast, north-east of Taipei – reported to be one of the wettest cities in the world. We were not surprised, therefore, when we ran into rain a few miles from the town.

But we spent a wet and fruitless hour in Keelung, while Kitty hopped in and out of the car making enquiries, to no avail! We could not trace the address and it was so damp and dismal that we decided the best thing would be to return home. We felt so frustrated, longing to find out where Jade came from yet getting nowhere.

Kitty went once more to the man who used to run the Home. The child's birth must have been registered at some office and if we could only find Jade's surname, we could no doubt trace her.

This time Kitty came back with not only Jade's full name but also the news that the previous Superintendent thought her birth would be registered in an office in Taipei. He had no idea where the people were who had handed Jade into the Home.

Nothing daunted, Kitty and I set out the following day, going from one office to another until, on the outskirts of Taipei, we found the office where Jade's birth had been registered. At last we had something to work on. We returned exultant, to be greeted by the new Chinese *amah* holding Jade in her arms. The child was crying bitterly, obviously upset.

'She no eat. You no here,' cried the *amah*, raising her voice to add force to her words. Then she handed the baby to me.

I took Jade into my room and began to feed her. She nestled down on my knee and hungrily ate all that I could give her. I kept her a little longer and soothed her before taking her back to the nursery.

She seemed all right, so I wondered why she had been so upset. She was not the only child that I took into my room from time to time. Another baby, a bit younger than Jade, Lily Lin, was also very insecure and so she too would join me occasionally when I was having a meal. I had scoured around the American bakeries in Taipei and found tins of condensed soup which I knew one or two of the babies would be more than willing to share with me.

Lily Lin and Jade would vie with each other whenever I took them both into my room, to see who could get closer to me. I became fond of all the children at the Home, but these two babies entwined themselves most firmly around my heart. So much so that the new *amah* we had employed only a week or two before, was sure that one of the babies looked like me!

The next time I went down to the town, she greeted me on my return with Jade in her arms.

'She your baby,' she cried. 'She same hair.'

I was very amused because unlike most of the babies, who had very dark hair, I had to admit that Jade's hair *was* lighter and rather like mine. But she was not my baby any more than all the rest. The only reason I had given her extra care, was because she was the most needy child in the nursery and cried so much. Now that the boils on her head were healing and she was being fed so well, she was certainly settling down more and was much happier.

However, the fact that I was very fond of her was undeniable. She had certainly stolen my heart. Could she become my baby? I wondered whether I *could* adopt her?

I dismissed the thought as suddenly as it came. It was so foolish! How could I adopt a baby? Single women just don't go around doing that sort of thing. Yet I must find out more about her. I knew her name, and that she was almost twenty months old. But further search would have to be delayed until after the weekend, for I was about to enter the hospital for the examination. In the last two weeks I had been tempted at times to worry about the possibility of having cancer, but I had immediately disciplined my mind and dismissed those dark thoughts. Had I not committed the whole matter to God? I repeated to myself a promise I knew from the New Testament: 'Don't worry over anything whatever; tell God every detail of your needs in earnest and thankful prayer, and the peace of God which transcends human understanding, will keep constant guard over your hearts and minds as they rest in Christ Jesus.'

As I 'hid God's word in my heart', His peace *was* keeping guard over my mind and heart. If my faith meant anything at all, it must be an 'oaken staff' on which I could lean just now when most needed.

Kitty went home, as usual, for the weekend which I spent alone with the staff and children. On Sunday morning, I was enjoying a leisurely breakfast in my room and sharing it with Jade and Lily Lin, when, suddenly, there was a loud knocking on the door. The original cook, whom we had been forced to dismiss, was standing there with two other men. As the cook began to shout and gesticulate, the Chinese woman who had let them in, translated: 'He want more money like *amah*.'

At first I was not sure what it was about. Then I realised that the *amah* we had been forced to dismiss, must have told the cook that she had been given two months' money. He had decided that he wanted the same.

I replied slowly in broken English, in the hope that I would be understood: 'He no can have more money. We have ninety-six children to feed. *Amah* has man in prison. She has four children.'

By this time, there was such a commotion that Jade and Lily Lin began to cry. I went back into my room to soothe them and returned to find the men getting more and more cross. I tried to reason with them while the

96

Chinese woman endeavoured to translate, but both babies were now yelling, so I again returned to my room to try to calm them.

As I returned to the door for the third time, I realised that I was not getting anywhere and might as well retreat. At least they were not in my room. So I went back to the babies and quickly turned the key from the inside.

The men were incensed as they realised what I had done. They began to bang on the door and shouted for all they were worth. My heart was pounding with fright! Whatever would I do if they broke down the door?

My lifetime habit of prayer came to the rescue and I called out in an equally loud voice: 'Dear Lord Jesus, please get rid of these wicked men.'

The men, hearing the sudden cry, went away much to my relief, so my prayer had been answered immediately! But they went outside and sat on a low wall in front of the Home, facing my window, glaring up from time to time for the next five hours. It was very unnerving. I constantly lifted my heart in prayer and they finally went away.

Immediately I asked one of the Chinese women to lock the outside door leading into the courtyard so that if the men returned, they would not be able to get in. Fortunately they never tried their luck again.

Jade and Lily Lin were so upset by all this, that it was quite some time before they stopped fretting and I was able to return them to the nursery.

The next morning I packed my bag with a few clothes ready to enter the mission hospital for two days. I waved goodbye to the children and took a bus to the town, then a pedicab out to the hospital.

The hospital staff were most kind and tried in every way to reassure me. Most of them were American but there were also Chinese students in training.

After a night's rest, my heart was full of peace as I was

wheeled into the operating theatre, for I knew that God was in control and that was all that mattered. The British doctor arrived. I was given an injection to put me to sleep and the doctor offered up a simple prayer. By the time he had finished, I was unconscious.

12
A matter of life and death!

When I came round later in the hospital ward, I wondered at first where I was. Then I realised that I was in fact in a hospital on the island of Taiwan. Not until a week later would I know the result of the examination under anaesthetic which I had just undergone.

The rest of the day passed pleasantly enough, the nurses chatting happily as they brought my meals. I wondered how 'my family' were, up at the Children's Home. I was longing to get back to them.

On being discharged next morning, I decided to get a pedicab to Gladys's home. My legs felt rather wobbly and it was too far to walk. I was disappointed to find that neither Gladys nor Yang So were in. We had not arranged to meet, as I was not sure what time I would be leaving the hospital. I turned away from her door forlornly. Even my pedicab man had gone, so there was nothing for it but to walk until I found another one.

Feeling decidedly 'under the weather', I slowly made my way along the lane between the neat little rows of houses, longing to meet someone I knew. Then I realised that the Chinese man coming towards me *was* someone I knew – Mr. Ding of the CAT Airlines. He was on his way to see Gladys, so I explained that she was not in.

'You don't look too well,' he remarked. 'Are you all right?'

I told him that I had just been in hospital for two days

and was not exactly bursting with life. To my astonishment, he put his hand in his pocket and handed me an American ten dollar bill.

'You look as if you could do with a good meal,' he said. 'Why don't you go and get something to eat, or at least a cup of coffee?'

Bless him! It was just what I needed. A kindly word from a friend and some practical help.

I warmly thanked my benefactor and made my way to the American Services' Restaurant. I felt strangely uplifted and thanked God for sending His servant just when I needed a human hand of encouragement.

After my snack I felt refreshed and got a pedicab to the bus station. I had not long to wait for the bus to Peitou and was glad to be going 'home' to the children. But it took me much longer than usual to walk up the mountainside. The scenery helped to cheer me on my way, for the azaleas were now in full bloom and I drank in their beauty. It was good to be out of hospital and in the open air again. I could hear the sound of the hot sulphur springs and, as I got nearer, I could see the iridescent colours of the fountains as the sun blazed down upon them.

Kitty welcomed me back and I was glad of the usual siesta that afternoon. Later that evening, we planned what we would do in the following days, for my time was at a premium. There was book-keeping to do, letters to be answered, news to be sent regularly to the Trust and to my family in Britain, and the children to be supervised and cared for.

I was getting to know 'my family' very well by now. Some of the eight to twelve year olds would often come into the store with Kitty and myself to help us sort through clothing which had been sent from the West. There were some lovely things, but occasionally we would come across something totally unsuitable. One girl dug her hand into a huge tea-chest of clothing and brought out a large black undergarment which she promptly tried on – to the shrieks of laughter from the others! In laughing together and living together, we all became firm friends. Indeed I forgot that they were Chinese. I loved them, and they understood the language of love better than any other.

Very soon Gladys came to visit us again. She would often spend a day with us when she was not tied up with speaking engagements or other matters. On one such visit, I enquired, 'Gladys, do you think the authorities would let me adopt a little girl and take her home?'

'I don't see why not,' she replied. 'They would not let you have a boy but I feel sure you would be allowed to adopt a little girl.

'Then I wonder if I *could* adopt Jade?' I said, at last expressing my thoughts aloud. It was quite obvious to me that Jade had adopted me, but the big question was whether I, in turn, could adopt *her*. And I did not dare consider this seriously until I knew what the position was regarding my health.

I longed to know the verdict. Meanwhile I made a point of not taking Jade out of the nursery more than I had to. I did not want the child to be heartbroken if I was not allowed to adopt her and had to leave her behind when I returned home. But I *did* continue to make enquiries about her. Kitty was of great assistance and Gladys was thrilled at the possibility of one of her little girls being taken home to Britain. If permission were given, Jade would be the first of her children to find a home in the West, and Gladys did all in her power to help me.

We finally discovered a Mr. Shu, who had placed Jade in the Home, and asked if permission could be given for me to adopt her. Mr. Shu promised to contact elderly relatives of the child who lived in the southern part of the island, and bring the answer back the following week.

In the meantime, I was praying about the matter. I asked God to make the way clear for me to adopt Jade if it was the right thing for me to do. I knew that first I would need to adopt her in the Chinese court in Taipei, so I prayed that this step would work out if it was right for me to take the child home. And then I waited.

Waiting is one of the hardest things to do in life. It is so much easier to work; but I reminded myself of another verse from the Bible which had been such a help to me throughout my life: 'I will instruct you (says the Lord) and guide you along the best pathway for your life; I will advise you and watch your progress.'

As I waited, God *did* advise me.

It dawned upon me that an incident, which had taken place just before we left Britain, might at this precise time have some relevance. The apparently foolish incident involved a letter one of our Cardiff secretaries had written to the Queen, five months earlier, asking whether Her Majesty could give her consent to Chinese orphans being brought into Britain, for adoption. We felt that it was not quite the thing to arrive home from the office one evening and just sit down and write to the Queen! Supposing everyone did this? In any case, we were caring for children in Taiwan and there was no question of trying to take them to Britain for adoption.

However, six weeks later, just three days before we left Britain, a reply had been received, via the Secretary of State: '... your petition of 28th October has been referred by the Queen to the Secretary of State, who, by Her Majesty's command, has given it consideration and has to explain that there is no objection in principle to individual Chinese or other foreign children, who are under fourteen years of age, coming to this country for adoption if satisfactory arrangements have been 'made for their care here ...'

102

The whole incident seemed no longer foolish, but terribly important. I sent a hasty airmail letter to our Cardiff friends asking them if they would send photostat copies of all correspondence connected with this question of adoption. But, until I knew about my health, I knew I could not take any definite steps to adopt Jade.

I began wondering again just what the future *did* have in store for me. Was I to be allowed to live, or would I have to face the fact that I might not be alive by this time next year? I thought again of the word I had received from God, some two years ago: 'I know the plans that I am planning for you, plans of welfare and not of calamity ...' With these words ringing in my ears and great peace in my heart, I went to see the doctor – to hear the result of the investigations.

It was a nondescript kind of day. At least it's not raining, I thought, as I wended my way down the hillside, waving to Kitty and some of the *amahs*. One of the latter had Jade in her arms and I wished the child could have accompanied me. But today must be faced alone without the companionship of those tiny arms clinging fiercely around my neck.

Alighting from the bus in Taipei, I took a pedicab out to the doctor's surgery. Changing my shoes at the door for the customary mules, I was relieved to find there were very few patients awaiting the doctor's attention that morning. My heart was beginning to pound and although I must have been waiting less than half an hour, it seemed an eternity.

How time can drag when we are facing a crisis! I wondered what my family were doing back home in England. Little did they know what mental pressure I was facing. I had not dared to tell them anything of my present ordeal in my letters, because Mother was not strong and any sudden shock or worry could prove fatal. Anyway, why worry my sister and the rest of the family when they could do nothing to help in a practical way? For the present, let them imagine that I was surrounded by happy Chinese youngsters, having some kind of a holiday in the sun-baked East.

Jim was the only person at home to whom I had mentioned my 'problem' and I had asked for his prayers. He had responded by sending me on tape the lovely solo from Mendelssohn's *Elijah*, 'O rest in the Lord'. He had no inkling this was one of my favourite pieces from the oratorio, and it came as a gift from God just at a time when I needed encouragement. I played it over many times in the days before my visit to the doctor, and felt strengthened and helped.

At last, the surgery door opened and it was my turn to see the doctor. As I entered, he looked up and smiled.

'Do sit down, Miss Porter,' he said, and not wanting to prolong the agony he hastily continued, 'I am sorry if I worried you, but you do not have cancer . . .'

Not giving him time to say more, I blurted out, 'Never mind, thank God!' as relief flooded my being.

He then went on to explain that from the human point of view, it had seemed an obvious diagnosis but, being a Christian man, he, too, knew the God who could heal, and we rejoiced together.

I left his surgery walking on air! Never had it felt so good to be alive. My heart was singing and I lifted my mind to God with thanksgiving. What did it matter that clouds were in the sky on a somewhat dull day, when my heart was bursting with thankfulness and song?

I couldn't wait to get back to the Home. Gladys would be coming up to see us on Sunday. What news I had for her! Also I really *could* consider the possibility of adopting Jade. My mind reeled at the exciting possibilities of the future. 'Plans of welfare and not of calamity,' God had promised. What more had He in mind for me?

13
Could I adopt her?

I burst into the old hotel and bounded up the stairs two
or three steps at a time. The joy in my heart provided the
necessary spurt of energy. I was at the beginning of a
whole new life.

I went into the nursery to see 'my baby'. As she caught
sight of me, out went her little arms, her soulful eyes
pleading to be picked up and cuddled. I swept her into my
arms and gave her a kiss and a hug as I whirled her
around, pretending that she was flying. Her beautiful face
lit up with the sunshine of a smile and she chuckled with
delight. *I* had been very firmly adopted; all I had to do
was to adopt her in turn!

But it might not be as simple as it seemed. I could
hardly stow away with her on a BOAC jet. I must adopt
her properly. It was complicated enough trying to adopt
a child in Britain; no doubt it would be ten times more so
in Taiwan.

I turned my attention to the other babies in the nursery. The *amahs*, about to give the babies their lunch,
were glad of the extra help. These youngsters eagerly de-
voured all that was offered to them! They had none of the
fads of many children in the West.

On leaving the nursery, I went up another flight of
stairs to the dining-room to see the rest of the family.
Eighty-eight little figures, seated on forms at long tables,
were for once comparatively silent as they wielded chopsticks and scooped rice, meat and vegetables as fast as

they could into hungry young mouths. Having finished one bowlful, they would hurriedly go to the end of the room to have their bowl replenished, not just once but two or three times if they were particularly ravenous. I walked around the room smiling at each group, sensing the bond that was between us, even though we could not communicate in the normal way.

Kitty had waited to have lunch with me and as soon as she realised that I had returned, went off to collect food for the two of us. She returned in a matter of seconds, with a huge bowl. No wonder the children had enjoyed their meal. Everything tasted particularly palatable today, I thought, as I deftly used my chopsticks. Of course, it was not the food that was different, but the fact that I had a new life before me, and could set about adopting Jade.

A few days later a letter arrived from Britain containing the photostat copies of the 'special' correspondence which our Cardiff secretaries had had with the Secretary of State. They had certainly been very quick off the mark in sending it out to us. I couldn't wait to go to Taipei to consult the British Consulate about the possibility of taking Jade home to Britain.

I went down to town as early as possible next morning, headed for the Consulate and asked whether I could see the gentleman in charge. It was not long before I was introduced to a kindly Mr. Barton. I explained my mission to him and showed him the relevant correspondence.

'What hope do you think there is?' I asked.

'With this correspondence, every hope,' he replied.

I said that I realised I must first of all try to adopt Jade in the Chinese court in Taipei. When and if this was accomplished, I promised to pay him a return visit so that we could set the wheels in motion for Jade to obtain a visa to return to Britain with me.

My hands were tied, however, until we heard from Mr. Shu, who had placed Jade in the Home. Would he *really* contact elderly relatives in the south? How long would he take?

I was not kept in suspense for long. The very next day, he reappeared. Calling Kitty to my aid, we managed to ascertain that the relatives had in fact given their permission for the child to be adopted. As I heard the news, my heart gave a hop, skip and a dance for sheer joy. Things were moving really fast now. Kitty and I arranged to meet Mr. Shu on the following Friday at the Chinese court office. Meantime, Kitty promised that she would obtain all the necessary forms. We could then present ourselves and the forms to the court and seek the necessary permission from the Chinese authorities for me to adopt 'my baby'.

Fortunately Gladys came to see us later that day, for it would be necessary for her to join us also at the Chinese court office. Permission would be needed from Gladys, of course, as the baby was in her Home. She gladly gave Kitty instructions about obtaining all the official forms.

Little did Jade know of all that was going on around her or the dramatic turn the future course of her life might take, in two or three days' time. As far as she was concerned, she was being fed regularly and experiencing what it meant to be loved and cared for properly.

Gordon was her special brother and when he came up to the Home with Gladys, she gave him a great welcome. He, in turn, would call for 'Dade' and he would bring little things to her in the playpen in my room. He knew there was something special about this particular little sister. Of all the ninety-six children in the Home, he had come to know this one very well and never forgot her name, though it was most difficult for him to remember the names of the others.

Gladys was delighted to know that we were all to meet on the Friday at the Chinese court.

'Do you really think the adoption will go through quickly, Gladys?' I asked. It would be a miracle, I thought, if it did. I knew of people in Britain who had waited a year or two years to adopt a baby from Hong Kong.

'I don't see any reason why it should not,' she replied. 'No-one has ever taken one of my babies to Britain before, so I don't *really* know. The only thing we can do is try.'

If it were left to Gladys, it would go through in no time at all. She never crossed her bridges before she came to them. Because sometimes, she hadn't always *had* a bridge!

I thought of the time when she had reached the Yellow River with almost a hundred children, on that epic journey across the mountains during the Sino-Japanese war, only to find that there was in fact no bridge. You can't swim across a river that size, she mused, and even if you could, you could never expect nearly a hundred children to do the same. Now she really was up against it!

There was not only no bridge, but there did not seem to be any boats either! For four days they had wandered along the bank of the Yellow River. First one and then another child would come to her and ask 'Ai-weh-deh, when are we going to cross the river?' When indeed! How could she answer them? She did not know herself. She had prayed and prayed that God would work a miracle. How could she reassure the children when her own faith seemed about to falter?

Then on the fourth morning, when she was tempted to despair completely, thirteen-year-old Sur-Lan approached Gladys with enquiring eyes and said: 'Ai-weh-deh, do you remember telling us how Moses crossed the

Red Sea and how God made the waters open up before the children of Israel?'

'Yes, I do, Sur-Lan,' replied Gladys.

'Then why doesn't God open the Yellow River for us?' enquired the child with utmost sincerity.

'Because *I* am not Moses,' said Gladys.

'But God is still God, isn't he?' the child argued. 'If He could do it for Moses, He could do it for us, couldn't He?'

For a few minutes Gladys was speechless at the audacity of the child's faith. Then a surge of joy and hope entered her heart, for had she not communicated her own faith to the child? Yes, the child had the very same faith in the very same God that Gladys had. The seed which Gladys had sown had come to fruition – the child meant every word that she said.

Gladys whispered, 'Let us kneel down and talk to God about it, Sur-Lan.'

As they got up from their knees, a Chinese soldier was approaching them. To say that he was amazed to see so many children in the care of one small foreign woman was putting it mildly. He could hardly believe his eyes! On hearing of Gladys's plight, he whistled loudly in the direction of the far bank of the river. In reply two small figures appeared pushing a boat into the water and rowing it across.

Three boat loads of children were ferried across the great Yellow River in this way, Gladys accompanying the last load. God had heard the prayers of Gladys and Sur-Lan. She was not Moses, but God was *still* God.

My mind was brought back from my reverie to the present moment. Yes, this was still the same old Gladys who had done such exploits for God on the mainland of China. She felt sure she could handle the Taiwanese authorities!

Before she left us that evening, we prayed about the

matter together. She explained to God exactly what was needed, just as if He were sitting on the chair next to her. Her praying was as natural as breathing. I had come to love these times of intimate fellowship.

As Kitty and I waved 'goodbye' to her, we reminded her of our meeting at 10 a.m. on the Friday.

'I'll be there,' she said. 'Don't *you* forget either.' We assured her that we certainly would not!

The next two or three days were spent in coping with the mounting pile of correspondence which was reaching us from Britain and the States. Friends all over the world had heard of our problems at the Home. They sent letters of sympathy or encouragement at the news of Gladys's heartbreak over the people she had trusted so implicitly. Gladys needed every bit of encouragement she could get. Along with the encouraging letters came letters from people blaming her for trusting the couple who had been left in charge of the Home. How cruel and unkind some people can be – usually those who know least about the situation. When she received such letters of condemnation, her wounded spirit was sorely tempted to give up.

'What is the use of trying?' she would exclaim. 'I tell you, Vera, I am finished! I am finished!'

'No, you are *not*,' I would reply. 'God has brought you through difficulties before, and He will bring you through again.'

When she was particularly agitated, I would insist that she took a hot cup of tea or coffee and lay down to rest. She would invariably get up feeling much better and ready to take up the fight again.

At the moment, her mind was fortunately taken up with the question of my adoption of Jade and the arrival of Kathleen Langton Smith in a week or two's time. She was sorting out clothes which had been given to Chi-Kuang in Britain and which he had now out-grown.

'Look – this little yellow nylon suit will be just the thing for Jade to go home in,' she said, as if it was all settled. 'Chi Kuang has grown out of it so you may as well have it.' Here was faith in action! She believed that everything would go through smoothly at the court.

It was not quite as simple as it sounded, however. When Kitty and I arrived with Jade at the Chinese court on the Friday morning, and met Gladys, we realised that Mr. Shu had not turned up!

Well, it was quite early in the morning, I thought. Perhaps he would arrive a little later. Gladys agreed when I voiced my thoughts, then added, turning to Kitty – 'You are sure you told him *this* morning, are you?' Kitty assured her that we had.

We waited, and waited. There was no point in going into the court office until Mr. Shu arrived and so we stood on the pavement outside. As the morning drew on and the sun rose, we became hotter and hotter, and more and more weary. Jade became fretful but I held her in my arms until she finally dropped off to sleep.

Doubts began to grow in my mind about Mr. Shu. Perhaps he didn't intend to turn up at all. Perhaps this was a sign that I was not to be allowed to adopt Jade. Questions chased each other through my mind.

In the end we decided we couldn't just stand there on the pavement all day. After two and a half hours we gave up and went for some lunch, feeling very disappointed. Whatever did I do now?

14
In court

During lunch we racked our brains to try to discover why Mr. Shu had not turned up. He had seemed so certain when he promised to meet us a few days earlier. Gladys was as mystified as we were, but she was not prepared to concede defeat.

'Oh no, you don't give up at the first hurdle,' was her attitude. 'You just go right on trying. We will wait a day or two and then we will try again.'

On the way back to Peitou on the bus, I thought again of all the many children Gladys had adopted on the mainland of China. Now she had another family here on the island of Taiwan and each child had a history all its own. If Gladys could get one of them a good home in Britain, then who knows how many more might follow! So she wouldn't concede defeat yet.

After the waiting in the intense heat, we felt utterly weary on our return to the 'old hotel', and more than welcomed the afternoon siesta. Jade was put in her cot in the nursery, Kitty went to her room and, as I lay in my office/boudoir, I tried to think out the situation.

I had been so excited during the last few days at the possibility of the adoption proceedings going through without a hitch, that after the morning's setback, my spirits were distinctly deflated. Perhaps the man never intended to return? Perhaps he thought that it was not worth all the bother just for a girl . . .

Now, if it had been a boy, he might have done something. This stemmed from the ancient Chinese tradition that the birth of a baby girl was looked upon as a disaster, whereas a boy was heralded with much joy and celebration. But they would never let me adopt a little boy, Gladys said. Yet if they had too many girls anyway, why not let people have them who would love and care for them? At this point, I dropped off into a sound sleep.

When I awakened, things did not appear to be so grey. I went into the nursery to collect Jade and we went for a walk up the mountainside. The heat was more bearable and huge multi-coloured butterflies gracefully flew from shrub to shrub, so big that one was apt to mistake them for birds. Catching the butterflies and pinning them to coloured leaves was one of the crafts of Taiwan. Gladys had often sent packets of them to schools in Britain much to the delight of the children.

After our brief walk, I got down to dealing with correspondence. Letters reached us from all over the world as a result of Gladys's tours in the last few years to Australia, New Zealand, Canada and America. I was well and truly lost in my work when I realised that Kitty had appeared at my door. She had someone with her.

No – it couldn't be! Yes, it was Mr. Shu! As I jumped up to welcome him, my heart leapt for joy. He and Kitty explained what had happened.

Mr. Shu had been away in the south to get written permission from the grandparents for the adoption, and had fully intended to be back that morning to meet us at the Chinese court, but had been delayed through no fault of his own. Despite that, he apologised profusely. I was delighted he had come and talked to him at length through Kitty. It was decided that we would endeavour to meet at the court on the following Tuesday.

The next few days flew by and on Tuesday morning I was up early. This was the day when I was to become a 'mother' for the very first time. It did not take long to deal with the necessary office business. Very soon Jade was attired in her beautiful green dress which suited not only her personality, but her name. 'Yu Ching,' I murmured softly to myself. 'Precious Jade.' What a lovely name! She chuckled with glee as I got her ready for the great day. If all went well, she would become Precious Jade Porter by its end.

When we arrived at the Chinese court office we were immensely relieved to see waiting, not only Gladys, but Mr. Shu. The latter bowed low as he greeted us and as it was almost time for our appointment, we went inside.

It was not at all as I had imagined. We were ushered into a large room and an important looking man greeted us. First of all he spoke to Gladys. Oh yes, she was well known in the city of Taipei. Had she not adopted Gordon only a few months previously and given him her own name of Aylward?

However, the proceedings were not to be over in a few minutes. The matter was far too important and in fact took several hours. Paper after paper was produced, to which signatures were added. Gladys and Kitty were the witnesses to the whole affair, and every time Mr. Shu and I signed they, too, added their names. In between there was much talking and explaining in Chinese and English. I was given a shortened version of the adoption proceedings in English. I signed that I was: "... willing to take over the complete responsibility of Yu Ching's living, education, marriage, etc.' Furthermore, I agreed to 'love her, protect her and discipline her as my own daughter ...'

Finally, Gladys took her *t,uchang* out of her handbag. This was a small ivory seal which lay in a beautiful case, at the bottom of which there was a special kind of red ink into which one pressed the seal before using it to stamp official documents. It was very personal and always guarded lest it got into the hands of anyone other than the person to whom it belonged.

I, too, had been given a *t,uchang* by Gladys, so now I produced mine, ready to seal the document. But there seemed to be some hitch. Even I could sense it, though I couldn't understand the language.

As the various paper had been signed, they had been taken away to be checked. Now another important looking official came from the offices with papers in his hands and a worried look. He had a brief and heated conversation with Gladys and then with Kitty and Mr. Shu. Everyone seemed to be talking at once. What *was* wrong?

Eventually, he turned to me and, through Kitty, said:

'I am sorry, Madam, I am afraid you cannot adopt this baby.'

'But why not?' I asked in utter astonishment.

'Your husband is not here with you in Taiwan to sign the papers,' was his reply.

I turned to him with a smile of relief, and explained, 'That's quite all right. I am not married.'

Now it was his turn to look astonished. Was he hearing aright? He obviously thought I was mad! Single and adopting a baby! Whatever for?

It was one thing for Ai-weh-deh to adopt babies right, left and centre, but quite another to allow any foreigner to do so. No, it wouldn't do at all.

Quite sure now that he should deter me, he went on, 'How do we know you are single? You had better go to the British Consulate and get a certificate confirming that you are not married.'

Gladys cheerfully came to the rescue. 'That's all right,' she said, turning to me. 'We will go around the corner to a café for a cup of tea, while you pop off to the Consulate. Then we will have lunch and come back to the court this afternoon.'

Her matter-of-factness dispelled any fears which I had.

We bowed low and left the official, assuring him that we hoped to return in the afternoon. He, too, bowed as he showed us out of the room. What would Ai-weh-deh be up to next, thought he.

I left the rest of the company in the café and hailed a pedicab to take me to the British Consulate. Kitty had written down the address so that I would not have any difficulty.

My mind was in a whirl! Whatever would my friends at the Consulate think? I asked my pedicab man to wait for me for the return journey and made my way into the office.

A pleasant looking secretary asked if she could help.

'Could I see Mr. Barton, please, if it is convenient?' I asked.

He must have heard my voice, for he appeared at once and I blurted out, 'Mr. Barton, would you mind giving me a certificate confirming that I am single?'

How the Embassy staff laughed! They did not get such requests every day and when I explained why I wanted it, they obliged immediately.

Intrigued by the possibility of one of Ai-weh-deh's Taiwanese children going home to Britain, they wanted to do all in their power to help.

The necessary document was dictated at once to one of the secretaries, who typed it out. Mr. Barton then stamped it with huge British stamps to give it the necessary importance for such an occasion, and I left the Consulate clutching my precious document, voicing my thanks for such instant attention.

Glad to see that my pedicab man had waited for me, I jumped into his vehicle and we headed back to the café.

I was more than thankful for the glass of China tea which I drank while Gladys and Kitty inspected my 'document' confirming my single status!

'Can you stay to lunch with us and return to the court

in the afternoon?' Kitty enquired of Mr. Shu. 'Yes,' he assured us. He was free and would gladly do so.

Another sigh of relief! It was essential that he should remain so that the complete adoption proceedings could go through without a hitch.

We had a very happy meal together. Then, feeling refreshed, we made our way back to the Chinese court office. Would the official really accept my important looking document, or would there be other hitches? I wondered.

We were again ushered into the large office where the official recognised us and came over immediately. I handed over my precious document to him. He read it and with a beaming smile, took Jade from Kitty's arms and handed her over to me.

'Yes, madam,' he said to me, 'you may now have the child. All formalities are completed.' With this he bowed low, and we knew that we were dismissed.

No mother could have been more thrilled with her first baby daughter than I was with my Jade. I walked out of the court office on air! This beautiful baby girl, whose arms were about my neck, was mine. I loved her dearly already and sensed her complete attachment to me.

Now that the first step had been taken, I had to take the next one. I would need to get a visa for my baby so that she could return to Britain with me. For this I went back to the British Consulate. They were delighted to meet my daughter and I showed off my lovely Jade to the staff. They couldn't have been more helpful about the visa. First one cable went to Britain and then another. We waited for what seemed an eternity, but was in fact only about two weeks. Still no reply.

'Do you think it would help if I wrote a personal letter to Britain?' I asked Mr. Barton.

'It might,' was his reply. 'There's no harm in trying.'

Away went a carefully worded letter with a pleading

last paragraph: '... As Yu Ching is now my daughter, Miss Jade Porter, I shall be most grateful if you will kindly issue a visa so that my daughter may travel home with me ...'

Then again we waited and prayed.

Meantime, we were expecting Kathleen to arrive any day. The Children's Home was looking much smarter now. When we had bought new bedding for Kathleen, Gladys had ordered seven two-tier metal bunk beds for the older girls' room. Then I found some lovely red and cream material in the store, which some American friends made up into curtains for our entrance hall. As one entered the 'old hotel' it looked much more cosy and lived-in.

Friends from the nearby American army base continued to help us decorate and do odd jobs. Two servicemen arrived to mend loose floor boards and the kitchen door, while American wives helped to sort out tea-chest after tea-chest of clothing in the store. Bill and Jan Timmis, who had been such a help in our search for Jade's official date of birth, came up regularly and another American family, the Winklers, were a wonderful help too and invited us all out to their home for a meal to give us a break.

It meant a lot to us to have this voluntary help, and the 'old hotel' rang with laughter as we worked together. Just as we were about to stop for tea after a particularly hectic day, the new beds arrived. It was so exciting that we forgot about tea and proceeded to put them up and rearrange the room for the older girls. By the time we had finished, we were having our tea at 9 p.m. – tired but very satisfied with our day's work.

As well as receiving help, *we* were also asked to help our Chinese friends. Professor Penney Tung, for example, of the China Youth Corps invited Gladys, then me, to speak to his young people.

I told them of my experiences in Capernwray Hall and of our aim to introduce young people, not only from Britain, to a living faith in Jesus Christ. They were obviously intrigued to hear of youth work in the West, and when Professor Tung took us to visit the latest youth centre recently opened just outside Taipei, I was equally interested in their work.

After this another request came: 'Could you please type out our China Youth Corps brochure?' asked the Professor. 'We would like the English to be corrected.'

I was delighted to help, even though it took a whole day and I was anxious to keep up to date with my own work. I was expecting to return to Britain soon, when Kathleen arrived.

On the day she was due in Taipei, Gladys, Kitty and I went to the airport with a small party of children to give her a warm reception. Unfortunately her plane had been delayed with engine trouble in Manilla, so we had to trail home again, feeling rather disappointed. Gladys was particularly put out and Kitty and I tried to cheer her up by saying that it was much better for the plane not to arrive, than to crash on the way and Kathleen be lost altogether.

Gladys could reach such heights; but she could also sink to great depths. She decided suddenly that the two *amahs* in the nursery were not doing their work properly and asked them to leave. In their place she sent up to us two old ladies. When they arrived, Kitty and I looked at each other. We both had the same thought: 'Oh dear, they are much too old! They will never cope with all the work. Babies can be so demanding.'

The poor dears were very willing but moaned and groaned the whole week. 'Our bones ache,' they said. 'The work is too hard.'

Then, out of the blue after only one week, they gave in their notice. I managed to persuade them to stay an extra night and meantime asked Kitty to phone a local agency

119

in Taipei to try to get two new *amahs* quickly. The agency obliged and sent two younger women on six days' trial.

By this time Kathleen had arrived, but as she had been very sick and overtired due to flying and the change of hours, she spent the first two days in Taipei with Gladys before coming up to Peitou.

It was such a joy to welcome her at last – another helper from the homeland. The next few days were spent in showing her the ropes and handing over all the book-keeping to her.

But still our problems were not over! We had asked the trustees at home to send money direct to Taiwan to pay for the new items, but there were complications. Although the Trust complied with each request as soon as it was received, it was weeks before any money filtered through the banks and reached Taiwan. Fortunately we were able to use the money recovered from the Super-intendent, and Gladys could draw on the account which she had in Hong Kong to which she had sent large sums of money for the work when she was in Britain.

So much expenditure on new equipment was needed because Mr. Wong had let the whole place go downhill when Gladys was in Britain. With the help of the Chinese staff the place had been cleaned up thoroughly before Kathleen arrived, apart from the Japanese *tatami*, on which the children were sleeping, which I was not happy about. A little girl had been brought to me one morning with bites on her face and ears. I discovered to my horror that there were lice in the *tatami*. I asked Gladys's advice and she promptly ordered gallons of disinfectant to try to get rid of the creatures.

Meanwhile, having seen the neat metal bunk beds in one of Madame Chiang Kai-Shek's orphanages, we felt that we should be able to afford to get the same beds for Gladys's Home. The older girls loved sleeping in their new

120

two-tier beds; the babies had their cot-beds. We decided that the rest of the children must have decent beds also. There was plenty of money in the Trust Fund, and we knew the trustees would send out extra money for anything which Gladys needed.

The next day, while the children were at school, all the *tatami* mats were taken out to the back garden, washed with strong disinfectant and left in the sun to dry. 'That should do the trick,' said Gladys hopefully.

We agreed to meet her later that day in Taipei so that she could order more beds; different coloured ones for each room – blue for the older children and green for the younger ones.

Kitty and I measured up the rooms and counted how many beds we would require. Soon we were looking around the shops in Taipei. Sadly, there were no big shops in Peitou, so we would have to pay for the beds to be transported the twelve miles to the Home. At last, Kitty and Gladys spotted a shop that sold beds, but such a large number would have to be ordered. They certainly did not have enough in the shop for us to buy there and then. This was just as well as it would give us time to obtain the necessary money from the trustees in England. Kathleen was delighted at the prospect of replacing the old *tatami* bedding, but in the meantime it would have to go down again. All the mats appeared to be dry, so back they went into the children's rooms, until the great day when the new beds arrived.

The mats did not, however, last that long! The very next morning children of all ages were sporting bites. The lice, furious at being disturbed, had their own back on the poor children! Gladys was away taking meetings so we couldn't ask her advice: nor could we consider the possibility of allowing the children to be eaten for a second night. There was only one solution: the *tatami* must be burned.

The cleaning man was called and Kitty explained what we wanted him to do. He obliged with alacrity and in no time at all, we had a huge bonfire from which not even lice could escape. We explained everything to the children also; they could hardly wait for their new beds to arrive.

Meanwhile, I was still awaiting the arrival of news from Britain about that very special visa for which I had applied.

15
Visas and vaccinations

It was Saturday and I was in charge of the Home. Gladys had asked Kathleen to join her in Taipei to attend a 'Freedom from Hunger' luncheon, so that Kathleen could meet local people of importance.

Kitty had gone home for the weekend as usual and it looked like being a peaceful weekend for me at the Home.

How mistaken I was!

Just as I was about to have lunch, two of the Chinese *amahs* appeared at my door with Peter who was just five months old. They were anxious because he did not seem at all well. I knew from experience that the first thing to do was to take the child's temperature, and I kept my thermometer by my side for such crises. Even so, it was a shock to discover his temperature was 103!

After a hasty lunch I got ready to take Peter down to the missionary hospital in Taipei, where we already had two children. I was about to order a taxi when some American friends appeared in their car. On hearing of the situation, they immediately offered to take me down to town with Peter. The hospital diagnosed gastric 'flu and decided to keep Peter in, but one of the other baby boys was much better, so he could accompany me home. Good news indeed!

The next day we held a dedication service for the new babies which went off very well, except for the condition of our youngest child, a little girl, barely three months old, who had been brought into the home very recently. She had not been at all well, with sores on her little body probably caused by malnutrition. Gladys named her Martha Aylward; however, because she was so tiny her nickname became 'Minnie Mouse'. Sadly, after the dedication, she seemed worse.

'I'll take her down to the hospital, I think,' said Gladys.

'It might be the wisest thing to do,' I agreed. 'Would you like me to book a taxi for you after lunch?'

If there was one thing I disliked doing, it was using the telephone. I usually picked up the receiver, then waited ages until someone replied. From then on it was a shouting match. I would shout as hard as I could into the phone; the person on the other end would shout back. Neither of us could hear and the strain was unbelievable. It was a wonder that anyone ever bothered to use the instrument. But it was the only way to call a taxi or the doctor, so one had to persevere!

At last, when I seemed to have been on the telephone for hours, I got the person on the other end to understand that we needed a taxi. Finally, Gladys, Gordon and Minnie were driven off to see our friends at the missionary hospital.

The next morning the gastric 'flu struck again. First it attacked me, and I reluctantly had to stay in bed all morning while Kathleen cared for me. Then by lunch time Kathleen was the next victim, so I got up and crawled around trying to look after her!

The next morning, feeling somewhat weak, we both tried to get back into our stride when the telephone went. It was Gladys, who seemed as if she were speaking from somewhere in Siberia, the line was so faint.

At last we were able to make it out: 'You will be sorry to know that Minnie Mouse died last night,' she said.

We were indeed sorry to hear that our youngest baby

had passed on. If only she had been brought to us earlier, we might have been able to do something for her.

But Gladys was still speaking faintly.

'What was that, Gladys?' I shouted. 'Can you speak up?'

'Yes,' she bawled down the telephone. 'Can you hear now?'

Assuring her that I could, she went on: 'I think Minnie died of a contagious disease. All the babies and children must be inoculated at once and the place fumigated.'

I noticed she didn't mention the adults. Her first thought was for the children.

'Do you know what disease it was?' I bellowed, conscious that any doctor who came to inoculate the children would want to know what he was trying to prevent them from catching.

'No, I can't remember what the hospital said it might have been,' she shouted back. 'They are taking tests this morning.'

'All right, we will get the doctor,' I assured her. 'Leave it to us.'

As soon as I came off the phone, I conveyed the message to the staff through Kitty and the flap began. First, one of the young teachers rushed down to the school and brought home all our children, who thought it was great fun to be interrupted in the middle of their lessons and told to go home. They tore up the mountainside and burst into the Home full of beans, while the teacher went on to contact the local doctor and a nurse in Peitou.

In the midst of all this, there was someone at the door.

I ran down the big stone steps, two at a time, into the front hall to try tactfully to put off any would-be visitor.

An old Chinese lady stood at the door, very agitated, who insisted on coming in. I took her upstairs so that

125

Kitty could translate and we could find out what she wanted.

'She says that Miss Aylward has sent her up from Taipei to help us,' said Kitty. So we guessed that Gladys, anxious to be of some help, had put her in a taxi, while she went to the hospital to get the results of the post-mortem on Minnie.

Our first task was to calm down the old lady, who was in quite a state. We assured her that all was well, and that we had sent for the local doctor and nurse. There was not really much that she could do but we did not want her to feel that we didn't appreciate her kindly offer.

Then back I went to telephone the hospital, knowing that it would take quite some time before I even got through. It was essential that we knew what Minnie had died of. At last someone answered.

'This is Gladys Aylward's Children's Home,' I bawled. 'Can you please let us know what disease our baby had – the one who was brought in to you on Sunday and died yesterday? Her name was Martha Aylward.'

'Pardon,' shouted a voice back, 'can you speak up, I can't hear.'

Again I tried, and at last I got the message through, only to hear the voice reply, 'I am afraid we don't know yet. We are taking tests this morning. Can you phone back please?'

The Chinese doctor and nurse had appeared by this time. The children were due for their regular cholera injections, so they came prepared for that. But on hearing about Martha's death, they decided to wait until the result came through from the hospital.

Everyone was on tenterhooks. The children were so excited at being brought home from school that it was difficult to keep them in order, so we sent them out into the open air to play until we needed them.

Again I phoned the hospital; again I was told to phone back.

The doctor meanwhile was getting more and more impatient; but at last, at my third attempt, I discovered that 'Minnie Mouse' had died – not from anything contagious – but of septicaemia.

No-one was more relieved than the doctor. He proceeded at once to give all the children their cholera injections. It took some time and as might be expected some protested, while others took it stoically. It was very hard work.

Kathleen was the worst affected, for she fainted! But it was the effects of the heat. The perspiration was just running off our bodies. She soon recovered, happily. But the excitement of that particular day was not yet over.

The doctor and nurse had left, the children were upstairs in the dining-room having lunch, when the telephone rang again. Who could it be this time? It took a few minutes to make out who the caller was.

At last I heard a voice saying, 'This is the British Consulate. Is that Miss Porter?'

I assured them it was.

'We have received a cable from England this morning,' the voice went on.

'Oh, what did they say?' I shouted.

'Just two words – Grant visa,' the voice replied.

'Oh, how wonderful,' I shouted back. 'I will come down to your office first thing in the morning. Thank you so much for letting me know.'

I rushed into the nursery, swept Jade up into my arms and said, 'You are *really* mine now, darling. We can go home to Britain.'

She didn't understand a word of what I said, but she enjoyed the jig which I did with her around the nursery and chuckled with sheer delight.

The next morning I couldn't wait to go down to the

127

Consulate to claim that precious visa. It was no effort to get up and I dressed Jade in her green dress which she always wore when going to town. I walked down to the bus in Peitou with her in my arms and soon we were in Taipei. By now I knew my way to the Consulate, where we received a warm welcome. As Jade did not possess a passport, a Declaration of Identity in Lieu of Passport was issued for her. It was an important-looking document giving her date of birth, 24th June, 1962, and stating that she was desirous of travelling to the United Kingdom 'to accompany her adoptive mother, and wishes to leave about 20th April'.

The visa was valid for two months. At the same time we were issued with a transit visa for Hong Kong, which permitted us to stay only two nights.

Before we could leave, Jade had to have another vaccination against smallpox at the quarantine station in Taipei to enable her to travel to Britain.

Meantime, Gladys was going from office to office with me; endeavouring to get an exit visa for me also. The problem seemed to be that on arrival in Taiwan, when my visa was checked for duration of stay, I had been given a resident's visa by mistake. Now that I wanted to leave the island it was not so easy. Gladys 'knew the ropes', however, and asked various friends to help.

As far as I was concerned, the Chinese characters in my passport meant little to me, so I had to leave this to Gladys to sort out. But it was awkward. Our provisional plane bookings for 26th March had had to be cancelled a week before we were due to travel, as it had been obvious we could not leave by that date. Further bookings were made for 29th April in the hope that our visas would be granted by then.

The waiting days passed very happily nevertheless. My birthday had come and gone and I had been presented with a piece of beautiful yellow embroidered material by

Gladys so that I could make a bedspread in true Taiwanese fashion on arrival home.

We went shopping, too, for appropriate clothes for Jade to travel home in and bought her a delightful pale green dress with a sailor collar. It had three pockets on the skirt from which three embroidered ducks' heads peeped. New shoes and socks were also bought and she was ready for her big journey into life.

Gladys loved taking me around the shops and showing off her beloved island. With her help I purchased very cheaply two pieces of dress material and the Chinese tailor, who did all her sewing, made it up into two sheath dresses for me very inexpensively. I had two lovely new dresses costing well under one pound each!

I had grown very fond of Taiwan and would be sorry to leave, but I was excited at the prospect of going home with my daughter. At long last our exit visas were granted. Gladys contacted one of her many friends on the Saturday before we were due to leave on the Monday and collected the documents. We were ready for our journey home. She suggested also that Jade and I should stay with her in Taipei for our last few days on the island. We had great fun, particularly with the children. Gordon and Jade were like brother and sister, and so enjoyed being together.

The black cloud of deception still hung over Gladys's heart, however. She could not get over the fact that she had been deceived by the very people she had trusted implicitly. For myself, I had done all I could humanly speaking and advised her to let the matter rest there and leave the issue in God's hands. I felt that my task was to return home now, set up the Trust office and raise as much money for her and the work as possible.

Monday morning, the day of our departure dawned, and I was up with the lark. Whatever happened I must not miss that plane.

I whipped one of my new sheath dresses out of the big wardrobe set in the wall. As I scrambled into it, something appeared to drop out on to the floor. I hastily turned around and discovered, at my feet, one of the biggest cockroaches I had ever seen. I shuddered. 'I only hope there are no more in the dress now that I am in it too,' I thought. I shook myself in the hope that any other would-be visitors to the homeland would be dislodged.

Soon Jade was dressed in her new dress and our cases stood ready at the door. Gladys and Gordon travelled with us to the airport with some members of the family. As we arrived we spotted Kathleen with a group of the children from the Home and other friends I had made on the island.

Esther Huang, Gladys's best friend, came up and presented me with a pink silk scroll inscribed with the following words:

To Dear Miss Porter:
   Having noticed you wan a victory for Lord, I present this valuable verse to you – Ps. 18: 29. God bless and keep all of you safe and sound. My love to you, your all families, friends for ever.
Lots of love to you,
Esther Huang

Then a Chinese business man gave me a beautiful porcelain lamp. When I expressed doubts about getting it home safely, he just said, 'Don't worry in the least. I will post it on to you.' 'Oh dear, it will get broken in the post,' was my passing thought. 'I don't suppose I shall ever see it again.'

Other friends were soon crowding around as well, handing me gifts, anxious to say goodbye: the missionary doctor, the friend from the air line office, some of Gladys's older sons, Jan and Bill Timmis and other American friends, Kitty and her mother, Kathleen and children from the Home. There were so many to speak to in such a brief space of time.

Finally, Gladys presented me with a beautiful Chinese visitors' book, the pages of which were interlaced with the most artistic black and white and coloured cut-out pictures. Inside, I discovered, many friends had signed it.

At last I had to tear myself away. I gave Kathleen and Gladys a hug, and went up the steps of the plane with Jade in my arms. She was clinging tightly to me, uncertain of what all the fuss and noise were about.

We took our seats. The great engines of the plane revved up and very soon we were airborne. My stay on that wonderful island was over but I had a very precious part of it with me – my lovely Chinese daughter. How would she settle in Britain, I wondered?

16
Church spires and cherry trees

After an uneventful hour-long flight from Taiwan, Michael met us in Hong Kong with a taxi and took us along to the YMCA, a small inexpensive guest house where the people in charge gave us a very warm welcome for our two days' stay in the colony.

Soon we were boarding the plane to take us home to Britain. A delightful air hostess took both of us under her wing, providing a carry-cot so that Jade could sleep at my feet whenever she desired. It was a long and tiring journey for a two-year-old and she voiced her protest, along with the other babies on the plane. The business men in our party were not the only ones to sigh with relief when our twenty-four hour flight was over!

The excitement rose within me as we landed at London Airport and stepped out of the plane into a refreshing breeze, though we shivered slightly, feeling the cold because we were tired. The wife of the Chinese friend in Taiwan, who had presented us with the beautiful lamp, greeted us and insisted that we spend the night in her home. We accepted gratefully, but first had to visit one of Gladys's best friends in London.

As we drove there in a taxi, everywhere I looked I could see church spires and cherry trees. This was England's 'green and pleasant land'; this was home and I was thrilled to be back.

Soon we were ringing the bell of a lovely flat in London's West End, where Helen welcomed us home as if we had been her own family. First we had light refreshments and then Jade was tucked up in a cot and I slept in a bed nearby.

Sleep was what we needed more than anything else, and Helen had the wisdom to see this. She was naturally dying to hear all about Gladys and Kathleen and the children in Taiwan, but she was very patient. After three hours, we both awoke feeling much refreshed and then our tongues wagged, as Jade played happily at our feet. A meal followed and we left to spend the night with our Chinese friend. She was living in London while her son was at boarding school in England.

The next morning we started the last leg of our journey home. At Euston we boarded the train for Crewe where my sister met us with Mark, her little adopted son aged four, who was thrilled at the prospect of having a new cousin.

Soon we were speeding through the country lanes of Cheshire. Buds were bursting on the trees, the sun was shining and spring was in the air. It was good to be alive and good to be back in Britain. Soon we came across more cherry trees and my mind went back to the lovely cherry trees in Yangmingshang Park just outside Taipei. Tourists made a point of visiting the area just because of the beauty of the trees. I had never realised until now that we, too, had our own 'tourist spots' in our country villages.

Ten miles outside Crewe we left the main road, turned off on to a side road and then left again up a long drive lined with rhododendron bushes. At the end of the drive we drew up outside a lovely old white manor house. We were home at last! Mother was there to greet us and delighted to be introduced to her new grand-daughter from the East. They took to each other immediately with the uncanny knowledge that youth and age so often have, that they have something in common.

Jade took it all in her stride amazingly well. She was completely used to hearing English spoken and settled down in her new surroundings immediately. They turned out to be a one-roomed flat with a roomy kitchen and a nice bathroom.

That was not all! Generous relatives and friends had seen to it that everything that could possibly be needed had been provided for the new member of the family. Our young minister and his wife had borrowed a cot and blankets, and had themselves provided a baby basket with everything that could be desired in the way of toilet requisites. My sister had lent us a carry-cot and high chair and various other things she thought we might need. It seemed to me that the love of God was very evident in this provision for one of Ai-weh-deh's children.

In the weeks that followed, as Jade and I travelled to schools, churches and all kinds of gatherings to show slides which I had taken, it was very evident, too, that there was just as much interest in the rest of Ai-weh-deh's children left behind in Taiwan. They very fact that Jade was there, seemed to bring home to school children and older folk alike the need of youngsters in the Far East. People willingly gave for the Gladys Aylward Trust and I often arrived back at the flat late in the evening, feeling exhausted, yet with a sense of great contentment. It was all so worthwhile.

School children in particular brought great joy to our hearts. We visited the Gregory School for Girls in Bradford and showed them pictures of their own little boy. How thrilled they were, and what a fuss they made of Jade. Fortunately she was too young to be spoilt by the attention lavished upon her. Wherever we stayed for the night on our travels, she accepted everyone as 'auntie' or 'uncle' and slept like a log.

I had to admit, though, that I was finding it difficult to

keep up with all the correspondence entailed in running the Trust together with speaking engagements, to say nothing of finding time to cook and do essential household chores.

There would be even more work to cope with soon, for I was to visit Jim in Scotland to take over the financial side of the work. Since Gladys's last visit to Britain and all the publicity in connection with her TV appearance, the work had snowballed. Jim had done a tremendous task but he must be relieved soon, for he had been working day and night.

There were also our Cardiff secretaries to thank. Now that the Trust office was to be officially run from my flat, all correspondence would come there in future. But how I was going to cope when everything was handed back to me, I just didn't know.

God, whose good hand was upon us, must have heard my unspoken prayer, for Joan Thomas, from Capernwray Hall, phoned one day. 'Could you do with any help, Vera?' she asked. My ears immediately pricked up. 'I have a letter from a Swiss girl who wants to join a family for three months to help as *au pair*. Could you do with her?'

'Yes, I certainly could,' was my reply. 'How soon does she want to come?'

'In about three weeks,' Joan replied. 'I will send her letter on to you.'

My mind was working overtime. This would fit in perfectly with our plans to visit Jim at the weekend in order to bring back to our flat the Trust work with which he had been coping whilst we were away. So we would be back in good time to meet our new friend.

I had purposely not booked up any speaking engagements for that week, and so we busily prepared ourselves for our journey to Scotland. It was an exciting thought! I would be seeing Jim again for the first time in seven months! My heart gave a joyous leap! But what would he think of my daughter, I wondered. What would she think of him?

It seemed no time at all before we were on the train speeding north to Scotland. Jim had arranged for us to stay at the home of a minister friend, who asked if I would speak at the church on the Sunday morning. I agreed with some trepidation! It was one thing to speak at schools and other informal gatherings, but the thought of speaking in a church on a Sunday morning rather scared me.

On our arrival in Dundee, Jim was there to greet us. Jade was introduced to him and from that moment he became 'Uncle Jim'. During the weekend they had high jinks as 'Uncle' pretended to wrap up the young lady in newspaper or made a newspaper 'coat' for her. Then there were visits to the shop around the corner with 'Uncle Jim' for 'tweeties'. He won her heart completely. I had a rival to share him with and, strange to say, I didn't mind in the least, for 'Uncle Jim' looked as handsome as ever and had not only stolen the heart of a small Eastern 'princess' but also the heart of an English lady!

Our time in Scotland sped by and it seemed that we had barely arrived when we were saying goodbye. Everyone had been so kind and the local paper, *The People's Journal*, had published a photograph of Jade with the minister's small daughter and a write-up about Gladys's work, which helped to bring in more money for the children.

Son after our return home, Marianne joined us from Switzerland. She made friends with Jade immediately and 'Mamiam' was taken to Jade's heart, too. We travelled happily together in my old Morris Minor to all kinds of groups to show slides of the work. In between, we had to spend several days at home in order to cope with the increasing volume of work. This was a good

136

sign, of course, for the more interest there was, the more money there would be to send out to our Far Eastern family.

Furthermore, there was a new issue of the magazine to be prepared. *Good Hope*'s last issue, printed just before we left Britain for Taiwan, had been much appreciated. Now friends were asking when volume No. 2 would be out.

Meanwhile, letters were arriving from Gladys and Kathleen, keeping us in touch with the goings on in Taiwan. Gladys wrote on 19th May: 'So sorry have not written, but things get so hectic and I started as soon as you went on my meetings so have been out most of the time. Everything is going on fine, Peitou is really moving. All the beds are there – new bedding coming in almost every day, painting, cleaning, etc., you will not know the place when you come next time. We miss you lots and Gordon walks in still to your room and says "Jade" and waves his hands "all gone". All sorts of people ask after you and we know you are as busy as anything . . .'

Kathleen wrote later, on 1st June, 1964: 'Enclosed please find monthly statement for May. You will see how I kept the payments low, for at the beginning of the month I was low in funds but have since received two lots of money for the Home. The balance was as you know 34,732.40 Taiwan dollars (approximately £72 sterling).

'By the way the dryer works very well and Gin is delighted. We have used it for three days now for it has done nothing but rain . . .

'I am fine now and just off to language school. Gladys is in good spirits, for she is out quite a bit and it is good for her. Give Jade a kiss for me.'

We were very relieved to know that the money was getting through at last. For, having been at the Taiwanese end myself, I knew how worrying and how frustrating it was to know that the trustees were doing all in their

137

power to send out the monthly allowance, only to find it was being held up going through the various banking channels!

Gladys, Kathleen and Michael also sent letters for *Good Hope* and it was such fun printing the magazine but, again, it meant the work piled up. When Judith, one of my friends, kindly offered to come and type for one or two mornings, her help was gratefully accepted.

By now, people from all walks of life were writing to ask if they could sponsor one of Gladys's children, and our office was expanding each day. Our one room proved far too small to be used as a living-room, bedroom and office, so when the flat across the corridor became vacant, we gladly moved in, for there was an extra room available.

Now we could have a little privacy in the large bedroom, though soon our living-room looked more like an office than a lounge or dining-room, with a big four-drawer filing cabinet in one corner, a large cabinet containing thousands of addresses in another corner, plus a drop-leaf table. A second-hand settee and two armchairs gave the room a more homely look and we were glad to sink into them on the rare occasions when we were able to relax at home.

The days and weeks sped by and Marianne had to return home to Switzerland. Other girls came to help on a short-term basis. Hanni, another Swiss girl, came to us; but after a week decided that she didn't like England.

'I only really came to England because I wanted to get away from my boy-friend so that I could decide whether I wanted to marry him or not,' she confided. Hardly the sort of news that would inspire confidence in her ability to help in this important work! Friends, hearing of our dilemma, assured me that their daughter would be pleased to help for a short time instead.

That was how Diana came. She was a great asset and as

her parents had expected, she loved the work and nothing was too much of an effort for her. When Diana first arrived, however, Hanni had changed her mind again! I certainly couldn't keep both of them! Finally, other friends came to my rescue and kindly took Hanni into their home.

Still, these small problems were nothing to those which Gladys was still encountering in Taiwan. All that we could do at the home end was to ensure that supplies of money still went out to her each month, and help to raise more for the Trust Funds.

Sometimes, our fund-raising efforts went awry. At one of the meetings at which I was showing slides, a journalist asked if he could take a picture of Jade. I agreed, for there had already been short reports in local newspapers when we had visited various schools.

I was not prepared for what happened, however. The over-enthusiastic reporter gave the impression in his article that we were waiting for people in Britain to *adopt* children in Taiwan. If he had said 'sponsor', he would have been much nearer the truth! No mention was made of the great difficulties in adopting children from another land or of the long wait, if it were possible!

The result was that we were inundated with telephone calls and letters from would-be parents. I patiently explained to each one that the report had not been strictly accurate. They could only *sponsor* a child. One dear couple even wrote: '... if you have three children in a family, don't split them up, we will adopt all three of them.'

Fortunately, as a result of this misunderstanding, we made many good friends, proof again that all things work together for good to those who love God. But I did phone the young reporter and object, telling him that he had raised hope in many hearts which could never be fulfilled. To give him his due, he was full of apologies and promised to give an amended report in his paper if he could come and take another photograph of Jade. I agreed, and the photograph was superb and the second report a little nearer the truth!

A small pebble thrown into a big pond causes many ripples. The next was a telephone call.

I picked up the phone as it rang one morning.

'This is the BBC,' a voice said. 'Is that Miss Porter? Can you come to Birmingham this afternoon and bring your Chinese daughter? We should like to interview you on the "Midlands at Six" programme.'

'I'm so sorry,' I replied after some thought. 'I'm afraid I couldn't possibly come today. I took my car into the garage this morning to be serviced.'

A good thing I haven't got the car, I mused. I wouldn't know what to say, anyway.

'Oh, we will send a taxi for you both,' the voice went on.

How could I refuse? It would be very good publicity for the work, and bring in more money for the children.

'Oh, well in that case, what time would you want to collect us?' I asked, hoping that a few questions would help me gather my thoughts and come to the right decision.

'The taxi would call for you at 3.15 p.m. prompt,' the voice went on. 'Please dress your daughter in her Chinese clothes.'

'All right,' I replied in a daze. 'We'll be ready.'

I put the phone down, knowing that God would show me what to say when the time came. But the rush didn't help! The taxi was late and we arrived in Birmingham just before 6 p.m. Then we were taken to the wrong television studio! The driver leapt into his taxi again and tore off to the other studio where we arrived just in the nick of time! Tom Coyne and one of his colleagues were on the doorstep looking anxiously for us.

'Quick, you are on any minute now,' he said.

We were bundled out of the taxi and rushed up some stairs into a studio. Cameras were everywhere.

'Please put Jade in that chair,' said Tom. As I did so, he gave her a beautiful teddy bear to play with. I tried quickly to smooth her hair but Tom called out, 'No, leave the baby. The programme is starting.'

I stepped back and watched the opening of the programme on a small monitor screen. In this way I was able to view my daughter's total lack of reaction to the pandemonium around her. She was completely enthralled with the teddy bear. First she held teddy out; then hugged it to herself with a gleeful little chuckle, just as the TV cameras swung around upon her. This was how the viewers were introduced to her in the programme, while Tom explained who Jade was. Then another person was interviewed before me, giving me time to smooth my hair and gather my thoughts. Eventually there was an informal chat with Tom before the cameras as I told of my work with Gladys in Taiwan. The programme finally faded out with Jade in the armchair still hugging teddy.

I picked her up and gently released her fingers from the teddy bear and left it on the chair. She looked a little surprised but did not object.

'No, give Jade the teddy,' said Tom. 'I bought it for her only this morning. Sorry I couldn't get anything else. I hope it is all right.'

'Are you sure?' I said. 'How kind of you. She would love it. Thank you so much.'

Jade expressed her thanks in her own way, her little eyes lighting up as teddy was returned to her. As a result of the programme, interest in the work soared.

17
The rough and the smooth

As a result of meetings, interviews and the publication of our second issue of *Good Hope*, we had managed to get all the ninety-five children in the Home sponsored. School groups or individuals paid five pounds each month for their particular child and received brief details of the child's date of birth, how it came into the Home and any other facts which we had been able to discover, plus a photograph. We still needed extra gifts, of course, for the maintenance of the 'old hotel' and new equipment.

After speaking at one Inner Wheel rally in Prestatyn, not only did the ladies give us a generous gift for the Trust funds, but for some weeks afterwards other donations came from other Inner Wheel clubs. The ladies had returned home to raise money in their own districts.

Just as the work was going smoothly, we were faced suddenly with a big disappointment. Gladys was told by the Japanese owners of the 'old hotel' that she must leave with all the children!

'What on earth is she going to do?' was my first reaction, for I knew from experience that the island was overcrowded, and the number of refugees going up all the time. 'And where will she find another suitable building to house a family of ninety-five?' With Kathleen and the Chinese staff, she would need accommodation for over a hundred. The only thing for us to do at the home end was to pray and wait.

The weeks went by. Day in, day out, Gladys made enquiry after enquiry but could find no building anywhere near big enough. Meanwhile, problems connected with the former Superintendent were dragging on and were a great worry to her. Gladys was very near to breaking point.

At last our prayers were answered, but not in the way we expected. An American organisation, the Christian Children's Fund, offered to take about seventy of our children. They suggested Gladys should keep only the younger children and babies, and look for a smaller building. She gratefully accepted their offer. Very soon suitable premises were found, and the babies and younger children moved into their new home.

I was relieved that the children had been re-housed, yet disappointed that we were losing so many members of our family. 'And, what about the sponsors?' I thought. 'Won't they be disappointed when they know we are giving up the children?' They would have become very attached to their particular children. Would they have to give them up?

Then a possible solution occurred to me. We could hand on the sponsors we had found as well as the children to the new fund. The suggestion was made and gratefully accepted. I comforted myself with the realisation that it did not really matter whether the money went out to the children through the Gladys Aylward Trust or through the Christian Children's Fund as long as the children were still cared for.

When all seemed to have been settled to everyone's satisfaction, the press in Britain got hold of the wrong end of the stick. Reports appeared giving the false impression that we had given up the children because of shortage of money, whereas we had plenty of money in the Trust funds. Other reports stated that Gladys was closing the Home completely. We were inundated immediately with telephone calls and letters from sponsors and friends asking for the truth.

On top of all this, the strain of the past year caught up with Gladys. Continuing problems with the former Superintendent, having to search for a new home for over ninety children, added to the wear and tear of a dedicated life, proved too much. Gladys became more and more confused in her mind, reliving the past as if it were the present, until she was not sure what was reality. She often seemed to be back in the days when I had worked with her in Taiwan.

So it was that stories about our difficulties the previous year began to appear in the press as if they were happening now – in the present. They were greatly exaggerated, making out that Gladys had lost everything and that she and Kathleen were having to scrub floors, which was just not true. It was no wonder that the public were confused!

Gladys's relatives were equally puzzled and wrote to us. They were receiving letters from Gladys which they could not understand at all. We tried to reassure them, explaining that the strain of the past year had been too much for her and they should not take too seriously what she wrote. Other friends of the Trust received very odd letters, too. Though we loved Gladys dearly and were continuing to do all in our power to help her, it was by no means easy.

Another problem reared its head. As new children came into the Home, Gladys decided to sponsor some of them direct with friends in the USA and Canada. But how could complete accounts be kept at either end if we did not know what was coming in, and when, for half of the children? It would have been different if there had been an office in America with which we could liaise. As we tried to find new sponsors in Britain for new children, someone in America might be offering to sponsor the same child direct with Taiwan.

This had actually happened with one Canadian lady and proved distressing for all concerned. We felt that we could not risk this happening again and tried to explain to Gladys that we preferred all the children to be sponsored through the official Trust office in Britain. Could not the American friends write to us?

In her confused state of mind, she could not see the point. She had no head for business and could not be bothered with accounts, simply because she did not understand them. God had given her another gift – she could tell a story and hold her audiences spell-bound. Now, however, she took hardly any meetings at all. She had done her work, and must be left to rest quietly. Never again would she be in the limelight. Her privations and difficulties down the years had taken their toll, and this latest nightmare of circumstances in Taiwan left her much older than her years.

In the end she gave up almost everyone at the British end. She did not reply to letters from friends, relatives or the Trust. There must be a suitcase full of letters somewhere in Taiwan, I thought, as we all tried to be patient and see the funny side. If only someone would rescue it and open the letters and reply as I had done when I originally began to work with her!

Knowing that she was not well, we stood by her. I continued to speak and show slides at all kinds of gatherings, and people gave generously to the work. Prayer partners were, however, anxious to have news, particularly as such odd reports were circulating. We sent out a prayer letter explaining that the situation in Taiwan was confused, and promising to let them have news when we found out what was happening.

The days and weeks went by. The weeks stretched into months, and in our little British office we were dealing with only a quarter of the children who had originally been in our care. The other three-quarters had been taken over by the Christian Children's Fund, and so had the sponsors. If new children were coming into the Home in Taiwan, they were being sponsored direct from America and we knew nothing of them.

I realised that, having done all the spade work and established the Trust, my work was now coming to an end, much as I loved it. As the work was now on a much smaller scale, there was no need for a full-time secretary/treasurer, or anyone to do deputation work.

The other members of the Trust felt as I did, so we asked if we could be relieved of our responsibilities when Gladys found someone else who would receive gifts and send the money out to her. We were very sad to have to do this, but felt that in the circumstances it was the best thing for all concerned.

Jade was now attending nursery school each morning and I was able to get on quietly with the office work. I had so much less to do, I no longer needed a temporary *au pair* or help with typing letters. Judith had been a tremendous help with the letters as she had faithfully worked away in the background all those months. I could not possibly have managed without her. A headmaster of a school snapped her up as secretary when we no longer needed her.

I began to think of what work I could take up when someone else was found to administer the Trust. Perhaps I could go back to the university nearby and take a part-time secretarial job until Jade was old enough to go to school? But my heart was still very much in the work amongst my dear Chinese children.

What did the future hold for Jade and me now? We did not know but we *did* know the God who held the future. He would not fail to guide us as wonderfully as He had done in the past.

As usual, I asked God's advice and received a wonderful answer as I read my Bible one day. A text jumped out from the page: 'Trust in the Lord ... verily thou shalt be fed.' It seemed as if God was saying to me: 'Stop worrying, I have taken care of you all these years as you have served me; I shall continue to do so. You are my responsibility.'

As I waited, God worked!

A few months previously, my dear mother had died. It had been a hard wrench to lose her. She had been a faithful warrior for God and had imparted her Christian faith to me at an early age. It was no doubt due to her influence and that of my godly father, that I turned my back on a rosy future in banking, to launch out in service for God. How privileged I felt to have worked at Capernwray Hall for almost twelve years and to have known and helped Gladys for about fourteen.

However, now that Father and Mother had passed on, some land my father had bought was handed on to my sister and me. As I was waiting on God, wondering how He was going to provide, a tiny bit of that land was re-zoned from farming land to building land and was sold to a local builder for a reasonable sum. At the precise moment when we needed it, God gave us help – not a moment before – not a moment late. Shortly after this, someone offered to take over the greatly reduced work of the Trust, and I could relinquish my responsibilities.

I had sufficient money now to get by until Jade commenced school in just over a year, when I could take a full-time secretarial job.

Soon we held our final meeting of the Trustees and Jim came down from Scotland. We were thrilled to meet him again, but I did wonder if it was to be the last time I would ever see him.

147

18
Bliss in Scotland

Jade was as delighted as I was to see Uncle Jim again, for they were good friends. When the final Trust meeting was over, he and I had time for recreation. We would walk the lovely winding lanes between tall hedges on our way to the village. Spring was here again, bringing new hope for the future to our hearts. We were emerging at last from a dark tunnel which had been full of problems.

All too soon it was time for Jim to return to Scotland. We said goodbye with the unspoken knowledge that a deep friendship had been forged in the trials which we had unitedly faced as we had sought to serve God as trustees of the Gladys Aylward Trust. We did not, however, make arrangements to meet again, but we wrote to each other regularly. Naturally I wondered whether our friendship would develop into something more. After praying for years that God would send the one of His choice for me, if it was His will, I was content to wait and let Him unfold the future one step at a time. Years before, I had become engaged to the wrong man – the agony was not worth repeating.

Letters arrived from time to time from Uncle Jim and when Jade was safely tucked up in bed in the early hours of the evening, it was pleasant to sit by an open window, with a gorgeous view of a well-kept and colourful garden, and to reply.

One night, when I had just put Jade to bed, the telephone rang. My heart leapt as I heard Jim's voice.

'What's happened?' he enquired. 'I haven't heard from you recently.'

'Oh, I was about to write to you this evening,' I replied – adding that I was delighted to hear his voice.

'Your letter is late so I became worried,' he went on. 'I thought that you or Jade might be ill.'

My heart gave a little dance for joy. So he was watching and waiting for the postman, was he?

'I would like to see you. Could you come up to Scotland for a few days and bring Jade?'

'Yes, we would love to,' I replied, 'when the friends who are staying with us have left.'

As I put the receiver down, the sun seemed to be shining right into the flat. I gazed through the window deep in thought, realising that the sun had long since disappeared! After that phone call, I knew something must be happening! But now I had to give myself the advice I had given my small daughter some time ago. We both had to wait until God told Uncle Jim what he had to do about it.

Our few days' holiday with Jim passed all too quickly. He was at school during the day, so Jade and I explored the neighbourhood on our own. In the evenings after tea together in Jim's sitting-room, there would be a story to be read from *Winnie the Pooh*. And we left Scotland with a promise from Jim that he would come to spend Christmas with us.

What a Christmas that was going to be! I was already planning the menus as we sped home on the train! The weeks passed quickly in all the flurry of Christmas preparations. The shopping was done, the tree was decorated, the presents were wrapped. All that remained was for Jim to join us in a few days' time. Then, two or three days before Christmas, came another phone call. It was Jim sounding rather distressed.

'Mother has had a heart attack,' he explained. 'She has had one or two mild ones in the past. We won't know the

149

full extent of the damage done by this present attack for a few days. I am torn between whether to come down to you as arranged, or whether to cancel my visit and stay with Mother.'

We talked for a long time. We both agreed that we should never forgive ourselves if anything happened to Jim's mother when he was away from her. No matter how disappointed we were, we must accept this setback. We could meet later on, when his mother was better. At the moment his place was at home with brother Norman and the rest of the family.

As I put down the receiver, a cloud descended about me. What a disappointment! But I reminded myself of George Müller's words, commenting on Psalm 37: 23. 'The steps of good men are directed by the Lord.' He said, 'Aye, but God guides our stops as well as our steps.' I was to realise the truth of this later.

Meanwhile it was very difficult for Jade at four to understand why Uncle Jim did not come to visit us at Christmas as he had promised.

Father Christmas came, however, and there was great excitement as Jade, Mark and Dawn (Jade's new cousin) enjoyed Christmas Day together and eagerly showed each other their gifts.

From time to time my mind would drift over the Border, as I hopefully prayed that Jim's mother would recover. God did not see fit to answer our prayers and took her to be with Himself some days later. Jim had done the right thing in staying at home.

In February he came down to us for a brief weekend during the school half-term. I could see that the loss of his mother had depressed him. He was restless, or would sit and play the piano and dream.

'Could we all three go away together on holiday in the summer?' he asked. So it was not nearly so hard to say goodbye, knowing we would be meeting again in the summer. We booked our holiday in a large guest house in Paignton and had a wonderful, and amusing, time because most of the guests took it for granted that we were married! Little did they know that we were only just beginning to get to know each other in a personal way.

To me they would say, 'I gave your husband your little girl's shoes; she left them in the garden.' Or to Jim, 'Are you looking for your wife? She's playing table tennis with your little girl.'

Jade adored playing 'tennis table' as she called it, though she was not much higher than the table!

The sunshine and beauty of the Devon countryside also did us a great deal of good. We were all three growing closer together every day.

The journey home was easy. Jade slept while we were travelling. She could switch off at will and go to sleep, which was a great asset.

Again came the goodbyes. Uncle Jim had to leave us to go back to Scotland, and I knew that I must continue to wait, though I found it very difficult. But it was made all the more worthwhile when I had a telephone call, a little while later, asking whether we could get engaged. Would I travel up to Edinburgh for a weekend so that we could meet and choose the ring?

My sister took care of Jade while Jim and I had a wonderful and never-to-be-forgotten weekend. He proposed properly and together we asked God to bless us and to continue to use us in His service.

I returned home with a song in my heart. My sister, Lilian, met me at the station with Jade. As I showed Jade my ring I explained that I had now become engaged to Uncle Jim. She could not understand.

'Engaged,' she said. 'But Mummy, I thought you could only be engaged on the telephone.'

I told her that it was not that kind of 'engaged' – I was going to marry Uncle Jim.

She shrugged off the news nonchalantly. 'Oh, well, that was my idea,' she said and ran to get into the car!

When Jim came down to us for Christmas some weeks later, Jade and he had great fun. He admired the gifts that Father Christmas had brought and we all agreed it was one of the best Christmases we had ever spent.

Some weeks later, on a snowy day in February, I travelled up to Scotland to look for a house. We were doubly fortunate, for we found the ideal thing and when we put in an offer, it was accepted straight away. There was only one thing wrong. Jade had specially asked for a house with a swing in the garden. Instead, the back garden was full of weeds two or three feet high and no sign of a swing. But that was easily remedied, and the lady in question was quite satisfied!

Our wedding day dawned – a lovely sunny summer's day in June. Jade and I had our hair done and got dressed. She looked beautiful with her gorgeous long black hair piled on top of her head; and as pretty as a picture in her white Swiss broderie anglaise dress and dainty head band of fresh white stephanotis flowers.

As I put the finishing touch to my case, Jade approached me with a question: 'Why can't I come with you?'

It was a reasonable enough question. She had accompanied Uncle Jim and me to Devon. Why could she not go to Switzerland with us?

Thinking quickly, I replied, 'Look darling, if you don't come on my honeymoon with me, then I won't come with you when you get married.'

Her little face lit up. She was quite satisfied, for her turn would come when she would, one day, wave goodbye to me!

Mark was the page boy in a smart Scottish kilt. They made a gorgeous pair as they stood together.

We had a wonderful service in the church which Jade

and I attended. We were very conscious of the presence of God as our young minister led the service; an old minister friend of Jim's (aged over eighty) prayed and Ian Thomas 'tied the knot'.

Our joy overflowed afterwards too, as we welcomed friends from far and near: Trygve from Norway, Catharine from France, a number of friends from Scotland and others from Wales and the south of England. One dear elderly lady was especially thrilled to be with us. Mrs. Sibley had written on our return from Taiwan, offering to knit garments for Jade. Dainty little handmade garments came through the post regularly and were much appreciated. Now we met the dear lady for the first time and could thank her in person.

We spent two glorious weeks in Switzerland. Jim wrote to Jade, signing his letter 'Daddy' and asking her what had happened to 'Uncle Jim'. With the help of my sister she replied that she was getting more used to calling him 'Daddy' and by the time he came home she thought 'Uncle Jim' would have got lost! And he did – he was Daddy from them on!

Jade's prayer had been answered for she had got her Daddy. We were out of the tunnel into daylight and the delights of our own home.

Only in retrospect can we see, with crystal clearness, that the wisdom of our Heavenly Father has guided us unmistakably in the right way. Even the deep trials, through which we all have to pass sooner or later, can become a blessing.

This came home to me recently, with great force, as I read the following beautiful verses in the Living Bible: 'When others are troubled, needing our sympathy and encouragement, we can pass on to them this same help and comfort God has given us ... to show from our personal experience how God will tenderly comfort others when undergoing these same sufferings.'

As a family, we cannot thank God enough for all that He has done for us. We shall ever be grateful to Him.

*　　　*　　　*

A year and a half after our wedding, we were sitting at home toasting our toes around a blazing coal and peat fire on a cold January evening, when our attention was riveted by an announcement on the television. A picture of Gladys appeared on the screen and we heard the news reader report that Gladys Aylward had died on that day, 3rd January, 1970, in her home in Taiwan.

As I listened, memories of Gladys crowded through my mind – the evenings when she had held hundreds spellbound in large halls all over the British Isles; that joyful 'This is Your Life' programme when she had sat on a studio chair, swinging her legs and clasping her hands like a child with excitement, as she was introduced to friends by Eamon Andrews – surely her shining eyes and beaming smile would never be forgotten.

Now this unpredictable, vivacious little woman had passed on. I wondered just how it had happened. I knew she had spent her last years quietly in Taipei, on her beloved island of Taiwan. As the year 1970 dawned, we discovered later, Gladys caught a bad cold, which seemed to take more out of her than it should. The doctor diagnosed 'flu and a touch of pleurisy and prescribed warmth and rest. When he promised to call again, he little knew that it was the last time he would see his famous patient alive. For, unexpectedly, during the night, the call came to higher service.

Kathleen, who still ran the smaller home for young children, had called to see Gladys and sensed that she was too poorly to be left alone. She decided to spend the night in her home. In the early hours of the morning, when she peeped in to see how Gladys was, she was shocked to find her dead.

154

The last chapter of her life had closed – yet her heart's desire had been fulfilled. She had died in the country of her choice, and would be buried amongst the people whose nationality she had taken as her own, in those far-off days on mainland China, when she had publicly burned her British passport.

Her main aim in life had been to introduce her fellow citizens to a living faith in Jesus Christ. Many responded and committed their lives to Him, and are today following in His footsteps, because of her.

Perhaps this sixteen-year-old's response by letter to the film and television programme about her, explains her special gift for inspiring others:

'I went to see a film "The Inn of the Sixth Happiness" some time ago. It affected me so much that for days I couldn't get over the fact that it was really true. It wasn't just a film. Through this film I was really and truly saved and I have been going to church ever since. Then I happened to see on a television programme, the very same person whom the film was about. There she was – real and looking so happy. I am writing this letter to say that I am now asking God to show me how to go to a Bible college or somewhere to learn more of His Word, that I may dedicate my life to Jesus Christ.'

*   *   *

And what now? Kathleen Langton Smith continues to work in the smaller Children's Home in Taipei, supervising the care of forty youngsters and taking meetings occasionally. Finance for this kind of work is constantly needed and God uses people from every walk of life to support His homeless, needy children through the Gladys Aylward Trust, which is still in existence.

Miss Ingrid Bergman, who took the part of Gladys Aylward in the film 'The Inn of the Sixth Happiness' continues to show a keen interest in the work of the Children's Home. She visited Taiwan in 1970 to find that Gladys had died only a short time before, so she never had the opportunity of meeting 'The Small Woman'. I met Miss Bergman myself not so very long ago. She expressed her joy at being able to portray Gladys's life but was sad that Gladys's prayer recorded in *The Small Woman* was not in the film: 'Here am I, God, here is my money, here is my Bible, USE ME.

Little Gordon, who was on the TV programme, has now grown up into a young man and is over fourteen years old. He is at school in the south of the island of Taiwan.

Gifts for the Gladys Aylward Trust may be sent direct to the Trustees in England at the following address – Gladys Aylward Trust, Messrs. Temple, Gothard & Co., 33–34 Chancery Lane, London WC2A 1EN.